"THE INVESTED LEADER"

(AND THOSE WE RAISE)

By

CATHERINE BROWN

Published by
The Transparent Publishing Company

Paperback ISBN 9781909805446

EBook ISBN 9781909805453

First published February 2018
Revised and updated March 2022
Original Copyright holder - Catherine Brown

Unless otherwise stated all Scriptures quoted are from Original King James Version of the Bible - Public Domain

TABLE OF CONTENTS

FOREWORD

In a day when many books have been written on the subject of leadership, **'The Invested Leader'** is special and stands out because of the perspective and understanding the author, Catherine Brown, brings to the book.

It is clear that good quality leadership will have a sustained impact over many generations. That is to say that if you are successful at leading, your impact may reach people who never even heard about you.

An invested leader invests in the people they lead; to them leadership is not simply a chore, but the pouring into others of their very life's essence. The invested leader devotes their time, resources, passion, and zeal into transforming the people they lead.

The author looks at the responsibilities of a leader not only from a practical but a spiritual perspective. A leader is a father, and a father is leader. The inheritance a father leaves to his sons (*not said in a gender sensitive way*) consists not as much in what he leaves **for** his children, but in what he leaves **in** them.

Jesus had a congregation of Twelve. These were the people He concentrated on and the people He poured Himself into. If you will nurture those you lead then you must restrict their numbers, Jesus was always available to the multitudes to heal and deliver them, but His leadership focus was always on the

4

Twelve, who in turn focused on the Seventy. As Catherine puts it, *"There must be a Kingdom relationship between the mentor and the mentored."*

As there are various kinds of fathers, there are also various kinds of sons and Catherine prepares the reader for what to expect and how to deal with the diverse challenges that are thrown up by divergent characters and personalities. There is the prodigal son, the orphan son, the rebellious son, the true son, and the list goes on. An invested leader acquires the skills and knowledge to nurture these diverse kinds of son.

Catherine also delves into some of the problems with fathers. She discusses immature fathers, absentee fathers, insecure fathers, abusive fathers, true fathers etc. and helps the reader identify the things that would make for better fathering.

Many have reduced fathering to 'tithe and covering,' that is, that in return for the son's tithe the father extends his spiritual cover to him. This demeans and diminishes the role of the father. The whole essence of fathering is to pass to succeeding generations all that you have received pertaining to God and His Kingdom. Like the author, I have no problem with a son tithing to his spiritual father, but it must not become the central focus of the relationship.

In her concluding chapter Catherine deals with the protocols of sending and of being sent. She broaches a very important subject here, since the church suffers from many who have called themselves and were never called by God and she deals with breaking ungodly protocols.

'The Invested Leader' is a must read for every leader or would be leader. I recommend it wholeheartedly and believe that it can transform the way we do Kingdom.
God bless as you read.

Wale Adefarasin
General Overseer
Guiding Light Assembly Churches, Nigeria

INTRODUCTION

"If we die without leaving a spiritual successor, then the seed of our spiritual legacy is lost."
Catherine Brown

When we are young, we do not give much thought to inheritance; we are simply little children living from day to day, unconcerned with the legalities and legitimacies that can accompany legacy succession and management. We have no thought of being an heir of anything and are more concerned with the kudos of being accepted by peers, teachers and loved ones than we are about inheriting anything from our parents.

Yet with the passing of time, all little children must inevitably grow up and eventually in the process of life they will lose loved ones and when this happens, the reality of being an heir of something or nothing becomes a part of the fabric of adult life.

When a parent does not make adequate plans to leave a physical legacy for their children after they pass away, their children inherit a huge heartache and, oftentimes, an equally large financial burden with large unmanageable debts for funeral expenses and other outstanding liabilities such as credit card bills or lapsed mortgage payments. The inheritance of such children is an horrific burden to all concerned.

Alternatively, when a parent intentionally makes appropriate plans to leave a legacy to their children, although there is the heartache and grief of parting, there is blessing in what is left behind as an inheritance both physical and spiritual. But of course we recognise that legacy is not only about what is left behind in death. Legacy is also about what we have *poured into others in life*. The paradox is that what we perceive in death is powerfully birthed and beautified in life.

This principle stands true for our physical children and for our spiritual children. This book focuses on what it means to be a spiritual parent and how we lead, love, and live with a mind set on legacy blessing and generational inheritance.

Blessed to be a Blessing

God has purposed that families should be blessed to be a blessing. God said to Abraham, *² And I will make of thee a great nation, and I will bless thee, and make thy name great; and thou shalt be a blessing:* Genesis 12

When God blessed Abraham, it was to be a material blessing for his family <u>and</u> for generations to come. *¹⁸ In the same day the LORD made a covenant with Abram, saying, Unto thy seed have I given this land, from the river of Egypt unto the great river, the river Euphrates:* Genesis 15

In the context of covenant God said to Abraham that the land was being given to his seed – his children, his heirs to come. The blessing was not for one man alone; that is not how God works. God blesses generations through fathers and mothers.

The fulfilment of God's promises included the material blessing of the land being handed down throughout Abraham's generations and it also included increase of the family itself as well as a spiritual legacy of blessing nations. *10 And the angel of the LORD said unto her, I will multiply thy seed exceedingly, that it shall not be numbered for multitude. Genesis 16*

Importantly, the Lord did not omit or forget Sarah in the confirmation of covenant blessing. He re-affirmed that the seed of Abraham and Sarah would be blessed beyond expectation, indeed that it could not be counted. Sarah, as a matriarch of the faith, is an example of the inclusion of women in the covenant of God in blessing nations.

Abraham and Sarah's legacy was:

Spiritual - Abraham was a Godly man with a righteous reputation and through his family line the nations would be bountifully and abundantly and exceedingly blessed!

Physical – Abraham, Sarah and their descendants were to inherit land. In addition to the spiritual blessings, their inheritance was also physical assets.

Biological - God promised Abraham and Sarah that their family and descendants would be so many that just like the stars they would be impossible to count and like the multitudes they could not be numbered.

This book focuses on generational succession and creating a spiritual inheritance from the perspective of Kingdom ministry/church and the task of raising up spiritual sons and daughters who will continue with the ministry. It is built upon the Biblical foundations of covenant blessing evidenced throughout the Old and the New Testaments and fulfilled in Christ and His church.

CHAPTER 1 - THE FATHER'S HEART FOR FAMILIES

14 For this reason I kneel before the Father, 15 from whom every family in heaven and on earth derives its name.
Ephesians 3 (NIV)

God created families for His glory and to reveal His Father's love, governmental order, and His blessing. The family unit is the place where we learn about identity, belonging and values. The Lord intended it to be a place of security, provision, and protection. It is our primary place to be nurtured and discipled as we are raised from infancy to maturity.

Family is the environment in which we learn accountability, discipline, and nurture. We learn to love and to be loved. We are taught how to share, how to be responsible, to accept delegation, accountability and to grow and be nurtured within the boundaries set for us under the tutelage of our parents or primary carers.

The family unit is the place where we discover our authenticity and in Godly functional families it is also the grace space where we comprehend our legitimacy. The core values that we learn in our primary family unit are the principles we will carry with us through life.

The church is a family of families that also must learn to model and outwork these same principles in the cultural mountains of the world for the Kingdom of God to advance powerfully in the earth.

No Dichotomy in Fatherhood and Governmental Rule

When Isaiah prophesied concerning the birth of Jesus Christ, he made the important statement that the government of God would be upon the shoulders of the coming Messiah.

Isaiah also said that the Christ child would be called, *6 b Wonderful, Counsellor, The mighty God, The everlasting Father, The Prince of Peace. 7 Of the increase of his government and peace there shall be no end, upon the throne of David, and upon his kingdom, to order it, and to establish it with judgment and with justice from henceforth even for ever. The zeal of the LORD of hosts will perform this. Isaiah 9 (NIV)*

Crucially, in Isaiah's prophetic declaration of the coming King of glory, there was no dichotomy between God's government and His Father heart. This principle stands true for eternity. In my observations from over twenty five years in ministry amongst Christian leaders I have found that too often leaders grasp only one of these elements at the exclusion of the other. For instance, some understand and model the powerful truth that God is Father, but they have little or no concern for His governmental power and authority and they are oftentimes confused in their thinking that the love of the Father cannot embrace a strong rulership grace. This is erroneous thinking because the legacy of the Father's love in His church cannot be separated from the wisdom of His ruling virtue and if it is we end up with impotency in leadership, and an accompanying inability to make difficult decisions or to set direction. In this scenario the people of God may well feel loved, but they will not experience being led if governmental grace is not evident in leadership.

On the other hand, I have met many other leaders who have received revelation and understanding concerning the governmental rule, authority, and power of Christ in, to and through His church, but conversely these leaders can sometimes end up being more dictatorial than acting as a spiritual father or mother! To rule without the love of the Father is to entirely miss the heart of God.

The truth is that both God's Fatherhood and His governmental power and authority are necessary for Kingdom rule and living. They are integral to governance; they are essential to right living on both a personal, church, and societal level.

I heard a story once of a young boy who was standing on the shore waving to a ship that was out at sea. An adult man who was near to him told him, "Don't be so silly, the boat is not going to change its course just because you are waving at it." The boy turned to him and smiled as the boat also turned and changed its course moving back to the shoreline. The man was perplexed and surprised as the young boy boarded and then shouted to him from the bridge of the ship, "Sir, I'm not a fool. The captain of this boat is my dad!"

This story blesses me because it speaks to us of the One who holds the destiny of the universe in His hands. He is our Heavenly Father and at the same time He has the power to govern our lives. He is with us always assisting us to navigate through the waters of life no matter whether those waters are calm or stormy.

Cultural (or Dominion) Mandate (Genesis 1:26-28)

27 So God created man in his own image, in the image of God created he him; male and female created he them. 28 And God blessed them, and God said unto them, Be fruitful, and multiply, and replenish the earth, and subdue it: and have dominion over the fish of the sea, and over the fowl of the air, and over every living thing that moveth upon the earth.

It is God's intention that families function as conduits for divine blessing and inheritance: both our nuclear families and our church families. In Genesis 1 we read of the cultural (or dominion) mandate. The blessing and the commission God gave to Adam and Eve, which is still relevant for families and for the church today in all its multi-faceted expressions and spheres of influence in the earth. It is reinforced by the Great Commission Christ entrusted to the Eleven and through them to the global church.

Let me make a brief point here. God included females from the beginning of His creation plans along with males. Someone recently tried to convince me (unsuccessfully I might add!) that God only thought of womankind at the physical creation and therefore, Eve was simply an afterthought and not necessary in the fulfilment of God's plans. Can you imagine! According to Genesis 1:27 *"created he him; male and female created he them."* This is before Genesis 2:21-:25 when God took a rib from Adam and created the woman Eve. We were created first in the spiritual image of God.

This flawed point of view of women being suggested as "superfluous" contradicts the Scriptures and is both dangerous and damaging to women *and* to men because it adversely affects our perception and therefore potentially limits or debilitates our outworking of the Cultural Mandate.

The cultural or dominion mandate is first released in and through the covenant of marriage and the family unit. It is also discharged through the church as men and women of God co-labour together in covenant together with God for the glory of God's Kingdom here on earth.

To operate in the fullness of blessing, we must realise we are blessed. It sounds an obvious thing to say but far too many Christians (and that includes Christian leaders) do not walk in faith, as a people who are favoured and blessed by Almighty God. If we know we are blessed, we will walk in authority and favour. Everything in our lives will be blessed: Our marriages, our children, our finances, our relationships, our health, our businesses, our homes and our callings and ministries all abundantly blessed.

We are made to bear fruit that will last for all eternity. Bearing fruit is a sign of a life truly changed by the good news of the Gospel of the Kingdom. As a result of the blessing of God upon our lives the Holy Spirit produces fruit in us to the glory of God. We are mandated for fruitfulness and appointed to bring forth fruit. Jesus reiterated this biblical principle when He said, *16 You did not choose me, but I chose you and appointed you so that you might go and bear fruit—fruit that will last—and so that whatever you ask in my name the Father will give you. 17 This is my command: Love each other. John 15 (NIV)*

Being fruitful is about increase and increase speaks of multiplication; God is not just promising that He will add to our "works and witness," but that He will grace us with fruitfulness and fullness in whatever capacity we serve Him and bring about supernatural increase and acceleration. The Kingdom of God is continually advancing therefore there can be no spiritual status quo for the family of God. The nearer we approach the Parousia (Second Coming of Christ) I believe we will see greater manifestations of God's glory in multiplication and acceleration of the things of the Kingdom of God on the earth.

I have been blessed as the Lord has multiplied time, resources, and money in my hands many times. I have seen money multiply, fuel in my petrol tank multiply, leaflets multiply and much more. Jesus Christ multiplied loaves and fishes to feed the multitudes and He is still in the business of taking the small and causing it to meet and exceed in miraculous proportions. All He needs is our faith and obedience. Christ has positioned us for maximum blessing.

Replenish means *to fill, refill, restock, reload, replace, stock up, top off and to up*. We can never run out of blessings or resource in the Kingdom of God because the Lord is the Source of all our provision in heaven and on earth. As believers we have the capacity to replenish people and circumstances in every walk of life. When politicians run out of answers, the church can replenish weary souls with the governmental grace, power, and authority of the Lord. When education runs out of answers, the church has wisdom and teaching beyond any earthly learning faculty; when the hospitals run out of medicines or doctors the church has the answer in the healing and miraculous power of Christ. When nations are in anarchy and the enemy has wrought destruction, the governmental wisdom of Christ will deal with systemic sin in nations and re-establish Godly order in the earth to restore peace and order to society. Whatever the situation we have the capacity in God to release the overflow of His love, provision, and governance to the world.

In Christ the fullness of God dwells; Jesus said, *21 that all of them may be one, Father, just as you are in me and I am in you. May they also be in us so that the world may believe that you have sent me. John 17 (NIV)*

As we remain in Christ, His fullness is released through us. As we disciple believers and our spiritual sons and daughters into places of influence and power in all sectors of society, God's glory and dominion will continuously fill the earth. Daniel said, *3How great are his signs, how mighty his wonders! His kingdom is an eternal kingdom; his dominion endures from generation to generation. Daniel 4 (NIV)*

As Christ's Kingdom ambassadors we are granted authority to exercise power on the earth and over all things created (both seen and unseen) in the name of the Lord, so that all enemies of God shall bow the knee in submission to God's reign and rule as His kingdom takes precedence over all.

We have been entrusted with authority and power on earth to advance God's Kingdom. We have this position in Christ, *15 Who is the image of the invisible God, the firstborn of every creature: 16 For by him were all things created, that are in heaven, and that are in earth, visible and invisible, whether they be thrones, or dominions, or principalities, or powers: all things were created by him, and for him: 17 And he is before all things, and by him all things consist. 18 And he is the head of the body, the church: who is the beginning, the firstborn from the dead; that in all things he might have the preeminence.* ¹⁹ *For it pleased the Father that in him should all fullness dwell;* ²⁰ *And, having made peace through the blood of his cross, by him to reconcile all things unto himself; by him, I say, whether they be things in earth, or things in heaven. Colossians 1*

Dominion

The cultural mandate of Genesis 1:26-28 specifically mentions 'dominion.' How are we to interpret this in our day?

Hebrew: 7287 Radah raw-dad a prim root; to tread down, i.e. subjugate; spec. to crumble off: - (come to, make to) have dominion, prevail against, reign (bear, make to) rule (-r, over), take.

What powerful language the Hebrew roots of the word 'dominion' reveals! We acknowledge the origin of dominion is in and from God, and the source of dominion is God. The Lord has dominion in all creation and over all things both in the seen and in the unseen realms. As believers we have been granted the **privilege, responsibility, stewardship, and authority of dominion as God's ambassadors on the earth.**

Dominion is also an aspect of divine legacy as we see evidenced in the Father/Son relationship between Christ and His Father. Jesus and His Father are one and the Father trusts Him with dominion over the entire earth. Jesus in turn has entrusted the disciples and the church with the mandate to disciple nations. *18bAll authority on heaven and on earth has been given to me, therefore go …. Matthew 28 (NIV)*

In this regard we simply place dominion in the context of the mandate or Cultural Commission that was given by God to mankind in Genesis 1:26-28 and which Christ reiterated/re-enforced with the Great Commission.

We have ever and always will be entrusted with the grace to disciple nations. *18And Jesus came and spake unto them, saying, All power is given unto me in heaven and in earth. Matthew 28*

CHAPTER 2 - JESUS - GOD'S SUCCESSION PLAN

[29] Lord, now lettest thou thy servant depart in peace, according to thy word:
[30] For mine eyes have seen thy salvation,
[31] Which thou hast prepared before the face of all people;
[32] A light to lighten the Gentiles, and the glory of thy people Israel.
Luke 2

Generational Succession Plan

Some four hundred years before the birth of Christ, Malachi prophesied about the turning of the hearts of the fathers to the children, and the hearts of the children to the fathers. According to Scripture if this did not happen, God said he would strike the land with a curse. *[5] Behold, I will send you Elijah the prophet before the coming of the great and dreadful day of the LORD: [6] And he shall turn the heart of the fathers to the children, and the heart of the children to their fathers, lest I come and smite the earth with a curse. Malachi 4*

Malachi was the last to prophesy four hundred years before the birth of John the Baptist, who was the cousin of Jesus Christ and a forerunner - a man like Elijah. Malachi is the last book of the Old Testament bridging into the book of Matthew, the first of the New Testament Synoptic Gospels. It is noteworthy that the significant message that connected the old to the new was that of generational succession. Jesus Christ came to reconcile us to the Father and to each other.

From the Old Testament oracle of Malachi we can summarise that if we do not operate with a generational succession mind set and plan for transition between the generations, God cannot and will not bring the fullness of His blessing. God's heart has always been, and continues to be, that the family unit would be blessed and be a blessing to the nations of the earth.

God's plan to save mankind is the greatest example of a generational succession plan the world has ever seen:

- In the provision by God to restore mankind after the fall - whereby man's independent action contrary to the will and instruction of God caused spiritual union and communion with God to be utterly broken until Christ's atoning work at Calvary
- In the miraculous and divine conception and birth of our Lord Jesus Christ
- In the sinless and perfect life of obedience and love of our Lord Jesus Christ
- In the perfect life, atoning sacrificial death, resurrection, and ascension of the Lord Jesus Christ.

Mary's Magnificat

Just three months after John had been conceived by his mother Elizabeth (Mary's cousin), Mary experienced a miraculous conception by the Holy Spirit, just as had been prophesied many centuries before. God in His sovereign wisdom brought forth His Son on earth through the overshadowing of the Holy Spirit on Mary.

In Luke Chapter 1 we read of Mary's response to angel Gabriel's message regarding the Christ child she was carrying and would presently give birth to. It is worthy of a meditative response on many levels. However, today we will consider "Mary's song" (or Mary's Magnificat as it is also known) from the unusual angle of generational succession.

*46 And Mary said, My soul doth magnify the Lord, 47 And my spirit hath rejoiced in God my Saviour. 48 For he hath regarded the low estate of his handmaiden: for, behold, from henceforth **all generations** shall call me blessed. 49 For he that is mighty hath done to me great things; and holy is his name. 50 And his mercy is on them that fear him **from generation to generation**. 51 He hath shewed strength with his arm; he hath scattered the proud in the imagination of their hearts. 52 He hath put down the mighty from their seats, and exalted them of low degree. 53 He hath filled the hungry with good things; and the rich he hath sent empty away. 54 He hath helped his servant Israel, in remembrance of his mercy; 55 As he spake **to our fathers, to Abraham, and to his seed for ever**. Luke 1*

On a personal level Mary praised the Lord, acceding to His rule and reign in her life. She praised God as her Saviour, recognising He alone was her strong and mighty deliverer. Her soul and spirit were in perfect unity praising God as she reflected on her future role as a mother to the beloved Christ child. Her humility had become a key to unlocking her destiny.

Significantly, we ought to note that the blessing God promised to Abraham and Sarah in the Old Testament is here affirmed in the New Testament by Mary at the divine conception of Christ. Mary specifically mentioned how God spoke to the fathers of the faith, to Abraham AND TO HIS SEED forever (see Galatians 3:16). We cannot fail to mention that the legacy succession plan of God through His covenant with Abraham is firmly evidenced in Mary's understanding and worshipful rhetoric.

Mary implicitly understood that God had a generational succession plan for all mankind and that the birth of the child, Jesus Christ, would ensure that God's mercy extended to all generations on earth. Mary chose God's way and embraced the call for the next generation. Mary's choices would bless generations to come. Mary's blessing had a 'now' application as well as a future legacy blessing too. Just like Mary, our choices affect not only our own destiny but those of our physical and spiritual children also. When we take on the role of being a mother or father it does not mean that we lose our personal blessing; instead when we choose to invest in the next generation the blessing will increase and manifest for the glory of God, whose heart extends to all generations.

For the believer, the covenant of marriage and ensuing intimacy are two essential components in physical reproduction. Likewise, to multiply in ministry the principles of covenant relationship with God and a close and loving relationship with Him are essential for fruitfulness - both in our own lives and in the lives of those we serve and mentor.

Mary understood that God was Israel's strong deliverer and that He was pouring out a generational blessing. God's mighty deeds include redemption, salvation, restoration, sanctification, healing, and deliverance through Christ, the child she would soon give birth to. God had in mind to bless all generations through His son, our Saviour, the Lord Jesus Christ, Son of the Living God.

The Bible teaches us that fear of the Lord is the beginning of wisdom and that it unlocks many other spiritual blessings and heavenly treasure for God's children. *4 By humility and the fear of the LORD are riches, and honour, and life. Proverbs 22*

God opposes the proud but gives great grace to the meek. If we try to build our own "empires" i.e. seats of power, influence and affluence, God will bring them down. However, if we endeavour to serve God in humility and to engage in advancing His Kingdom, then we will see His blessing extend to each generation. If we only build for our own "reputation" and self-edification, it creates a powerbase of selfish ambition with narcissist leadership - instead of fathers and mothers who build up their children and advance the Kingdom of God. Self-centred, egotistical leaders do not rear spiritual children - they create spiritual orphans i.e. converts with no father who will not pursue their inheritance because they do not see themselves as legitimate.

It takes humility and God-reliance to reach out and nurture the next generation. It takes Godly wisdom to mentor and train emerging leaders. **It is an act of self-effacement and a gift of great love to give oneself to raise up a son/daughter.** God our Heavenly Father gave us all in Christ; Christ the Son gave Himself fully for mankind in the love of His Father. If we model this lifestyle of loving and giving, then we will have sons and daughters who will give themselves in surrender to the work of God continuing to raise others also. If we invest in developing sons and daughters who carry our spiritual DNA, share our heart values, understand our vision and who have been discipled by us then we will leave a spiritual legacy to them and through them that will bring much glory to God.

I am not speaking here from a rhetorical perspective, but from my ministry experience of walking with those I mentor including my spiritual sons and daughters in the nations for many years, in various capacities. I am not teaching something I have not lived or continue to live by. The principles of spiritual parenting are deeply embedded in my DNA and life and ministry experiences.

Jesus About His Father's Business

The Lord continually made references to the fact that He was about His Father's business. *36 But I have greater witness than that of John: for the works which the Father hath given me to finish, the same works that I do, bear witness of me, that the Father hath sent me. John 5*

Jesus taught, *6 Blessed are they which do hunger and thirst after righteousness: for they shall be filled. Matthew 5*

Spiritually hungry people are God-reliant and depend on His goodness, grace, faith, and mercy. They are faith-filled individuals who seek God's face and endeavour to live fruitful lives, building teams that are competent and capable of achieving goals together.

On the other hand, self-reliant leaders operate with a mind-set of what they can do for self, and what others can do for them, rather than in the mind-set of how we can serve God and what God alone can do for us. Humble leaders are first Christ-centred, then others-centred rather than self-centred.

Provision for Spiritual Legacy

Jesus Christ was intentional about cultivating the next generation of leaders. He poured himself into His twelve apostles and authorised and empowered them to do the work of the ministry that His Father had entrusted to Him and which He then delegated to those whom He had trained as disciples. Likewise we must identify, invest, delegate, coach and mentor then release and deploy people to their full capacity in the fulfilment of their duties.

The disciples embraced what the Lord had modelled to and for them. On the Day of Pentecost Peter stood up in a loud voice and proclaimed the Gospel message, *38 Then Peter said unto them, Repent, and be baptised every one of you in the name of Jesus Christ for the remission of sins, and ye shall receive the gift of the Holy Ghost. 39 **For the promise is unto you, and to your children**, and to all that are afar off, even as many as the LORD our God shall call. Acts 2*

Provision for Family

On the Cross Jesus made provision for His beloved mother, *26 When Jesus therefore saw his mother, and the disciple standing by, whom he loved, he saith unto his mother, Woman, behold thy son! 27 Then saith he to the disciple, Behold thy mother! And from that hour that disciple took her unto his own home. John 19*

Kingdom leaders must recognise the need to foster other leaders by developing them. Apostolic intentionality is required to put a generational succession plan in place. If we are not purposeful about creating such a blueprint, our spiritual legacy will go to the grave with us and all that we have worked for will die with us. A generational succession plan is a blueprint that will ensure our spiritual legacy continues for generations. God has always been and will ever be a tri-generational God of blessing.

Generational succession in this instance simply means having a lifestyle that considers the next generation with intentionality in lifestyle and a transitional strategy in life and ministry to promote and advance the next generation of spiritual sons and daughters - and implementing that strategy so that the spiritual legacy for which you have laboured for together is not lost, but continues as a God-given blessing from generation to generation.

CHAPTER 3 - LEGACY

26 For ye are all the children of God by faith in Christ Jesus.
27 For as many of you as have been baptised into Christ have put on Christ.
28 There is neither Jew nor Greek, there is neither bond nor free, there is neither male nor female: for ye are all one in Christ Jesus.
29 And if ye be Christ's, then are ye Abraham's seed, and heirs according to the promise.
Galatians 3

Legacy

A legacy is something handed down by a predecessor (or an amount of money or property left to someone in a will). It is an alternative word for inheritance, i.e. that which a legal heir will inherit. For the purpose of our study we are considering what it means to create a spiritual legacy. What are we "handing down" to our spiritual sons and daughters?

Legacy is how we invest in others, and the fruit in their lives that is produced through that investment, which becomes a catalyst for further growth in a future generation of believers. Creating a spiritual legacy is first about who you are before it is what you do. Legacy is about Kingdom life and how you live and how you love, not about your death and retirement. Legacy is about how you invest your time, your talents, your finances, your wisdom, and your knowledge to raise others, not so that we can boast but that Christ is glorified in the flourishing and fruitful relationships we cherish and nurture.

Lineage

Lineage means ancestor or pedigree; No matter where we have come from in our lives with regard to social standing, money, education, status (or lack thereof), when we come into God's Kingdom as believers, we have a royal lineage through Christ. Apostle Peter writes that we are a chosen people, a royal priesthood, a holy nation, and a people who belong to God. (See 1 Peter 2:9)

In the natural order to receive one's legacy, a person must first acknowledge and understand their lineage. It is significant that the entire human genealogy of Jesus Christ is embedded in the opening chapter of Matthew, beginning, *[1]This is the genealogy of Jesus the Messiah the son of David, the son of Abraham: Matthew 1 (NIV)*
Proper understanding of spiritual lineage is established in our true identity, found in and through Christ. It is also essential that an heir is mature to inherit the fullness. Maturity and stewardship go hand in hand.

Heir

An heir is a legal inheritor and can possess their inheritance. In understanding and acknowledging lineage, there is a natural progression to accepting and acquiring one's legacy. Without understanding one is a legal heir, there is a danger that legacy could be "lost." Illegitimacy can affect a person's ability to claim their inheritance. In the Body of Christ today there is an alarming number of people who do not view themselves as being spiritually legitimate. This means they remain in a stagnant place in respect of maturity in discipleship, and regarding entering the fullness of destiny in their own lives.

Additionally there are those in the body of Christ who have remained spiritually immature, and they are not able to possess their inheritance because they lack maturity. Spiritual parents must address both issues of illegitimacy and immaturity in those they disciple. We are exhorted to raise mature sons and daughters – not babies!

Jesus said to his disciples prior to his death, *[18]I will not leave you as orphans; I will come to you. John 14 (NIV)* The disciples were not physical orphans so the Lord must have been addressing the issue of being a "spiritual" orphan, i.e. one who has not yet received the full revelation of the Fatherhood of God and/or who has not yet been fully adopted by the Holy Spirit into the family of God. The logical conclusion is that if a person is not a legitimate son, then they can never become a legitimate heir. Jesus wants us to inherit the Kingdom of God!

Through His death and resurrection the Lord Jesus Christ has reconciled us to our heavenly Father. It is through our covenant relationship with Him that we become legitimate partakers of the inheritance Jesus

Christ purchased for us at Calvary. We are heirs of God and co-heirs with Christ. *15 The Spirit you received does not make you slaves, so that you live in fear again; rather, the Spirit you received brought about your adoption to sonship. And by him we cry, "Abba, Father." 16 The Spirit himself testifies with our spirit that we are God's children. 17 Now if we are children, then* **we are heirs—heirs of God and co-heirs with Christ,** *if indeed we share in his sufferings in order that we may also share in his glory. Romans 8 (NIV)*

As believers we are in the wonderful condition of potentially receiving every spiritual blessing by faith in Christ. Apostle Paul's words to the church in Ephesus confirm this, *3 Blessed be the God and Father of our Lord Jesus Christ, who hath blessed us with all spiritual blessings in heavenly places in Christ: Ephesians 1*

John the beloved writes that from the fullness of God's grace we have each received one blessing after another. It is one thing to know about these spiritual blessings, but it is another to possess them. We must engage our faith to receive the blessings of God. They will not just drop into our laps, but they are ours to freely receive by faith. When we understand our position in Christ, we will be able to receive every spiritual possession and blessing.

LEADERS AND LEGACY MANAGEMENT

Spiritual leaders, spiritual parents and mentors may each be considered a type of "legacy manager" A primary role of a "legacy manager" i.e. the visionary leader of the family, church, ministry, or organisation is to:

- Establish and lay foundations, for there can be no successful or successive building work that will last without a proper foundation being laid by the spiritual father/mother of the house.
- Build according to the pattern! The legacy manager will have been entrusted with a blueprint or a pattern from God which will have within it the strategy for successful completion of the assignment, the house, or the ministry.
- To build and to advance God's Kingdom, encouraging and equipping emerging leaders in training to also be part of this process. The legacy manager does not only train a person for task but is interested and intentional in discipling and making spiritual investment into all team members, disciples, those they mentor and their spiritual sons and daughters.
- To nurture the next generation of leaders. It is essential that leaders are intentional about developing others to fulfil potential and Kingdom destiny.

As the Lord's people we must build according to the pattern. Building is a function of apostleship (see 1 Corinthians 3:10a). The generations must learn to work effectively and fruitfully together! A team can accomplish much more together than an individual

can. We all need a blueprint but before we can build effectively. Our blueprint is our vision from God:
Vision > Mission > Purpose > Mobilisation > Kingdom Advancement

Just as in the natural, construction work can be messy, tiring and often does not go according to the planned timeline or budget, so it is also with spiritual construction dynamics. In other words things do not always go smoothly.

I am grateful for the blueprint of the life of Nehemiah, an apostolic reformer in his day who had the capacity to look at devastation in his nation, see beyond with eyes of faith to restoration and to pull down from heaven the God-given strategy to bring solutions to the problems of the burned down gates and broken-down wall of Jerusalem in a supernatural period of 52 days!

Yet even Nehemiah faced opposition in his assignment and had to endure mockery, false accusation, prophetic manipulation and more. People threw proverbial stones at him. Perhaps at this juncture it might be prudent to point out that to be an effective Kingdom builder, one must develop the ability to lay a firm and strong foundation with the "bricks" that others throw at them!

Nurture

In addition to building functionality, leaders and spiritual parents must learn how to nurture others and help them grow. For this to take place a leader must create:

- A blueprint with clear, cohesive, and achievable aims and objectives that have been mutually agreed and understood as the plan of action.
- A route or course of developmental practises through which the leader in training can gain more experience and at the same time can be assessed in their leadership skills. Through such a process it will reveal how the mentee responds to challenges, successes, and failures.
- A "position" from which the trainee leader is able to progressively stretch their faith muscles and grow and experience first-hand leadership challenges and "live" management and/or ministerial situations.

Nurturing must make room for true delegation of authority and give room for the person in training to grow in skills, experience, and gifting. It has been my experience that you do not know how people may react and cope with authority until you give them some authority and power to exercise. The results can be illuminating! Abraham Lincoln once said, "Nearly all men can stand adversity, but if you want to test a man's character, give him power."

I have observed how the character of an emerging leader in training is revealed through trials, testing and temptation. Each of these stages is necessary for character development. A future leader must pass through the proverbial valley to be able to sustain and maintain consistency in leadership on the proverbial mountain top.

What Should We Take Into Consideration?

Relationships

There must be a genuine Kingdom relationship between the Mentor and the Mentee. Discipleship is relational and without it we can never truly get to know the gifting, strength, or weakness of another person. Neither is it possible for us to accurately assess how that person is developing and maturing if we do not have relationship.

As the person being mentored grows there should be unambiguous evidence of discipleship maturity and their life and witness. The senior leader must have the skill set and the maturity themselves to be able to identify leadership potential in others and help them develop and grow. Knowing a person's gifting, personality and potential is essential in placing them in appropriate roles.

It is important to see how your mentee responds to others in relationships, e.g. family, ministry etc. Does the person have a good balance in life and in ministry? Is the person accountable, submitted, teachable and loving? Is the person a team player? Are they a team builder? Can they be trusted with power and authority? Can they prioritise and effectively manage time and people? Are they reliable? Are they consistent? Are they committed? Can they set goals and achieve objectives? Do they have good personal foundations? Are they able to be under authority and operate in authority? Are they responsible and caring? Do they take care of their spouse and children? Are they self-aware?

I have learned through more than twenty five years in the ministry that trust is an important part of any relationship. **The fact is that you will not and should not promote a person that you do not feel you can trust.** It takes seasons of journeying together for trust to be both developed and tested. Sometimes the testing of trust and power reveals tremendous character, but sadly there are times when it reveals the opposite and character "defects" rise to the surface. Whatever the outcome the testing in the arena of trust is an important aspect of legacy planning and pruning. Either way the process is necessary.

Strategic/Visionary/Apostolic/Prophetic

It is paramount that the person you plan to promote (and/or appoint as your successor) must share your vision, values, and heart. You cannot teach 'heart,' as this is something that is modelled and 'caught' through sharing of life and ministry as it bears fruit in the leader's life.

Ministry is not only built on vision, but it is also constructed upon values, which are our Kingdom principles in ministry and every walk of life. A spiritual child should take on some of the spiritual DNA of their parents in like manner to a physical child inheriting some of their natural parent's genes. It is ever true that we reproduce who and what we are ergo let us seek to imitate Christ in all.

Character and integrity should be evident in all areas of life and ministry, including stewardship of finances and the person in training should be committed to prayer, personal devotion, and study of the word. Before God we are all equal, however, we need to understand that we *are not* all the same.

It is essential that we take time to observe the character, commitment and calling of a mentee <u>before putting that person into a position of responsibility</u>. Do not be tempted to put a family member in place if they are not equipped for the role simply because they are family. Instead think about the skills, gifts, talents and experience the person has for the job before you put them into place. If the person is called into ministry, they will have grace for every challenge that they will face.

Putting the right people in the right place will cause progression. However, placing the wrong people in the wrong place will cause regression, and having the right people in the wrong place will cause stagnation and frustration.

Crisis

Challenging times can provide tremendous opportunity for character testing and refinement.

Every leader-in-training needs to experience crisis and learn how to manage, transition, and respond through it. To reach the "mountain tops," we cannot by-pass the important lessons and principles that the "valleys" of life and ministry teach us. They give opportunity for "back bone" and resilience to be developed in us.

Crisis management teaches us faith, strength by grace, God reliance, humility and much more and we gain valuable life experience also. In times of trial we learn how to endure. Our minds are trained to stay focused on task and hopefully we become more Christ-like in character as we pass through difficulties learning valuable lessons to take with us for future life application.

(Acknowledgement: Apostle Naomi Dowdy)

CHAPTER 4 - MANAGING TRANSITION

21 Then said Jesus to them again, Peace be unto you:
as my Father hath sent me, even so send I you.
22 And when he had said this, he breathed on them,
and saith unto them, Receive ye the Holy Ghost.
John 20

Transition means change, changeover, evolution, conversion, shift, move, switch, alteration, and modification. All ministry has various times and seasons of transition. Within ministry we need to create a transitory period for legacy succession which should include:

1. Intentional development of leadership potential in upcoming/emerging leader(s).

2. Purposeful delegation of authority and responsibility to leader(s) in training with support from the apostolic leader. A type of "co-regency" like the King David and Solomon model may be a viable Kingdom Biblical example of two generations working together in a period of "hand-over." Mentoring is still required at this stage.

3. After a suitable period of training, the emergent leader should be fully released into their assigned position in the ministry and into their remit of authority and anointing. The mantle, anointing and authority of the new leader should be affirmed by the outgoing leader and

the incoming company whom the leader will serve.

Moses and His Generational Succession Plan

Moses found himself in a most distressing situation; he was a man alone in desperate need of creating a team with whom he could share the workload. Moses was an apostolic father, and as such he needed to raise spiritual sons and daughters with whom he could co-labour in the Kingdom. Nonetheless, it took Moses' father-in-law Jethro to point out to him the obvious – it was too much work for one person, and he needed to raise up the next generation of leaders to assist him in the ministry and work of the Lord.

13 And it came to pass on the morrow that Moses sat to judge the people: and the people stood by Moses from the morning unto the evening. 14 And when Moses' father-in-law saw all that he did to the people, he said, What is this thing that thou doest to the people? Why sittest thou thyself alone, and all the people stand by thee from morning unto even? 15 And Moses said unto his father in law, Because the people come unto me to enquire of God: 16 When they have a matter, they come unto me; and I judge between one and another, and I do make them know the statutes of God, and his laws. 17 And Moses' father in law said unto him, The thing that thou doest is not good. 18 Thou wilt surely wear away, both thou, and this people that is with thee: for this thing is too heavy for thee; thou art not able to perform it thyself alone. Exodus 18

The Strategy

[19] Hearken now unto my voice, I will give thee counsel, and God shall be with thee: Be thou for the people to God-ward, that thou mayest bring the causes unto God: [20] And thou shalt teach them ordinances and laws, and shalt shew them the way wherein they must walk, and the work that they must do. [21] Moreover thou shalt provide out of all the people able men, such as fear God, men of truth, hating covetousness; and place such over them, to be rulers of thousands, and rulers of hundreds, rulers of fifties, and rulers of tens: [22] And let them judge the people at all seasons: and it shall be, that every great matter they shall bring unto thee, but every small matter they shall judge: so shall it be easier for thyself, and they shall bear the burden with thee. [23] If thou shalt do this thing, and God command thee so, then thou shalt be able to endure, and all this people shall also go to their place in peace. [24] So Moses hearkened to the voice of his father in law, and did all that he had said. [25] And Moses chose able men out of all Israel, and made them heads over the people, rulers of thousands, rulers of hundreds, rulers of fifties, and rulers of tens. [26] And they judged the people at all seasons: the hard causes they brought unto Moses, but every small matter they judged themselves. [27] And Moses let his father in law depart; and he went his way into his own land. Exodus 18

Moses did exactly what his father-in-law had suggested. It took a father figure i.e. spiritual parent to point out the need for a generational succession plan. Apostolic fathers and mothers are strong advocates of raising up the next generation of spiritual sons and daughters and have the wisdom, insight, and oversight to release strategy for Kingdom management to their prodigies.

Tactical Implementation

Don't stop leading! Jethro encouraged Moses to continue to be an apostolic leader before God on behalf of the Israelites. Just because we are training others up does not mean that we stop leading.

Moses was to **teach** other potential leaders what he knew. Passing the baton to the next generation includes sharing and investing in them what we have learned in life and in ministry.

Moses was to show them how to live; as an apostolic father he would become a **lifestyle model** which they could imitate. We must never ask others to do what we ourselves are not willing to do.

Moses was also to **instruct** them in their duties and obligations teaching stewardship and responsibility. People do well when they understand what their assigned duties and role involve. As the leader communicate clearly to your team what you expect from them and dialogue with them over expectations. This type of open communication prevents misunderstandings at a later stage.

Jethro told Moses to choose **"capable men."** Moses needed to make an assessment on the potential for leadership in others and then nurture and develop them. In the quality of selectiveness, Moses chose those who had exhibited some **competency** in leadership prior to be appointed into a position of responsibility.

The **character** of the leaders-in-training was of utmost importance i.e. they were to be honest, trustworthy and God fearing. We do our leaders a deep injustice if we only train them for task; we must also develop their characters.

Each appointee was to be **assigned to a particular sphere of influence**; some were given delegated authority over tens, some fifty men, others hundreds and finally those with the capability and character to take care of thousands. As the senior leader we must be able to ascertain what level of responsibility a person is capable of undertaking at any given stage in their development.

The leaders were given **delegated authority** and could serve as judges, but Moses was to remain on hand to give counsel, wisdom, and insight to his team and to deal with the difficult cases. This was a time for generations to operate together in gifting, calling and experience. Delegating to others often requires degrees of transitional involvement by the delegating leader to the leader in training.

The leaders were to learn how to serve. The Lord Jesus taught that leading is NOT about lording it over others. The most effective way we can train others to serve is by serving.

As a result of the measures Moses took to share the apostolic work, the load became lighter, more effective, and far reaching and the team shared in and operated under an apostolic mantle. In this way the work got done and a new generation of Kingdom leaders was raised up.

We might summarise the process of Moses' leadership development plan along the lines of:

Affirmation i.e. recognition of leadership potential within trainee leaders

Activation into leadership i.e. release in relationship by a mentor to leadership development and discipleship.

Revelation and teaching i.e. impartation of knowledge and understanding.

Lifestyle modelling is a powerful tool in developing others in character and leadership potential. Effectively we are saying, "Do what I do" not just what I say. I try to ensure I take a spiritual son or daughter with me when I travel on ministry. If that is not possible, then I am usually collaborating with spiritual sons and daughters on the ground when I reach the nations. This means that our interaction is up close and personal. They get to witness first-hand how I live, how I pray, how I teach/preach, how I interact with others, how I conduct myself in all of life situations. They also get to be real with me, to share time as we travel and eat together.

Impartation – when we pray and lay hands on another, we impart revelation, anointing, release gifting, and call forth mantle and/or pass on a mantle (see Elijah and Elisha, *The company of the prophets from Jericho, who were watching, said, "The spirit of Elijah is resting on Elisha. And they went to meet him and bowed to the ground before him." 2 Kings 2:15*)

Please do not be hasty on the laying on of hands. I love this aspect of ministry, but I am considered and careful as to how and whom I lay hands upon.

When I commission a spiritual son or daughter as an apostle, or I ordain leaders into another ministry office I make meticulous plans as to how I pray and what spiritual gift I am imparting to them by the grace of God and the power of the Holy Spirit. When I commission a son or a daughter as an apostle, I pray for an impartation of part of the apostolic mantle I carry in Christ to be given to them. This is a weighty mantle and must be governed with diligence and due care. I am therefore vigilant as to how I administrate such a prayer of impartation. I caution all leaders to do likewise, whilst at the same time encouraging all leaders to lay hands on others by the unction of the Holy Spirit to stir up their spiritual gifting.

Delegation into a specific sphere/role i.e. assigned duties within context of calling and gifting. When people know what to do, they will perform the tasks assigned to them far better than when they are unsure of what those duties are. It is good when delegating to discuss expectations both from the perspective of the one delegating and the one being delegated to. This initial discussion on expectation makes it easy to do follow-ups and review as time passes.

Release into fullness of office/mantle/calling. Fullness comes with times, seasons, and experiences. It comes with stepping out and taking a first step of faith and continuing the journey of faith when passions wains. We live in a "microwave" society, meaning everybody wants everything fast. In leadership we may experience seasons of 'suddenly,' that accelerate God's purposes and plans in our lives, but we cannot expect to mature overnight in our calling without walking through process to enter promotion.

Truly the father or mother of the spiritual house makes spiritual decision that will affect the next generation! As leaders we have a responsibility to PASS IT ON!

[8] So now I charge you in the sight of all Israel and of the assembly of the LORD, and in the hearing of our God: Be careful to follow all the commands of the LORD your God, that you may possess this good

land and <u>pass it on as an inheritance to your</u>
<u>descendants forever</u>.

⁹ And you, my son Solomon, acknowledge the God of your father, and serve him with wholehearted devotion and with a willing mind, for the LORD searches every heart and understands every desire and every thought. If you seek him, he will be found by you; but if you forsake him, he will reject you forever. ¹⁰ Consider now, for the LORD has chosen you to build a house as the sanctuary. Be strong and do the work. 1 Chronicles 28 (NIV)

CHAPTER 5 - NO SUCCESS WITHOUT A SUCCESSOR

¹So when David was old and full of days, he made Solomon his son king over Israel.
1 Chronicles 23

There can be no true success in ministry unless we raise up a successor in our spiritual sons and daughters. Spiritual parents must be concerned with raising their children in the faith and encouraging them and empowering them to go further than they have. Jesus modelled this very principle, when He taught His disciples that they would do *even greater works* than He had done, because He was going to the Father (John 14:12).

The Scripture narratives concerning King David and his sons give illumination as a reference point for us to consider in ministry succession, particularly as we encounter David towards the end of his reign and his natural life on earth.

King David has become old and needed a blanket to be kept warm. In his dotage he had become self-serving instead of serving his people. He was no longer operating as a priestly king. What a sad change from the man of God we encounter on the threshing floor, who builds an altar pleading for his people and the mercy of God.

King David requested that a search be made for a virgin, and a beautiful girl was found who took care of the king and waited upon him. *⁴ The woman was very beautiful; she took care of the king and waited on him, but the king had no sexual relations with her. 1 Kings 1 (NIV)*

The king was in a fruitless relationship; whilst it was not an impure relationship, nonetheless it did not bear fruit to the glory of God. A king should bear fruit; kings are rulers and rulers are legacy builders. The people were concerned about finding comfort for their king. It should be the other way round – a king is raised up to lead his people, to build nations and to bring comfort, wise counsel, and action in times of need and national crisis. A true king should not be concerned about the status of sitting upon a throne. A true king is more concerned about serving the people through whom the throne grants him access.

Preparation for Legacy Management

¹²He gave him the plans of all that the Spirit had put in his mind for the courts of the temple of the LORD, and all the surrounding rooms, for the treasures of the temple of God and for the treasures for the dedicated things. 1 Chronicles 28 (NIV)

My son Solomon is young and inexperienced. The task is great, because this palatial structure is not for man but for the LORD God. With all my resources I have provided for the temple of my God. 1 Chronicles 29:1/2a (NIV)

David had previously prepared for succession by collaborating with his son Solomon on preparations for the temple to be built. David had shared the vision blueprint and resources with his son, and it would seem there was an intention at some point to hand over the throne, since David had entered a time of co-regency with his son Solomon.

Solomon was not thrust into the position of king without being prepared by his father. In fact they enjoyed a time of reigning together, before Solomon eventually acceded to the throne to rule by himself with his father's blessing. This is an essential principle in mentoring. We must exercise wisdom in how we first train, equip, coach, mentor and delegate to task and positions of power and influence.

As spiritual fathers and mothers it is essential that we invest in our spiritual children in every way possible. We have equity they do not yet possess. We have experience, we have assets both spiritual and physical and we have wisdom and counsel they desperately need (whether they realise it or not). God may have given us a blueprint as He did to David, but it may be that we are to empower the next generation to build what God has revealed to us, just as it was with King David and his son Solomon.

David's dreams and vision were shared with his son along with the values that had become the foundation for his rulership. Together, the father and son team participated in management of Kingdom legacy, preparing for hand-over as they led together until the time for the young king to take over his father's throne. This is a great model.

When runners are taking part in a long-distance relay race and they are passing the baton from one team member to another, it is necessary for the two runners to run alongside each other for a time to pass the baton. At the point of passing then the forerunner can run on ahead. The transition of the baton happens through the correct approach, synchronicity of timing, shared focus, trust, and teamwork. It is necessary for one to run ahead and then another to come on board and run alongside at the appointed time. The baton must be released from one person to another person. It does not pass itself. Both team members are needed for the race to continue.

However, something happened that seemed to interfere with the succession plan. Despite his best intentions, David had temporarily dropped the baton rather than passing the baton on. As a result he was late in handing over the throne to his inheritor. This delay caused chaos in the interim period until things were properly resolved.

Adonijah – Heir Apparent

Because of this delay, his son Adonijah stepped up and put himself forward, *⁵ Now Adonijah, whose mother was Haggith, put himself forward and said, "I will be king." So he got chariots and horses ready, with fifty men to run ahead of him.* 1 Kings 1

Adonijah was heir apparent (his three elder brothers were dead). But God had promised that it would be Solomon and not Adonijah who would be king as successor to David. The throne had already been promised to Solomon, *¹³ Go in to King David and say to him, 'My lord the king, did you not swear to me your servant: "Surely Solomon your son shall be king after me, and he will sit on my throne"? Why then has Adonijah become king?'* 1 Kings 1 (See also1 Chronicles 22:9 (NIV)

Surprisingly, David did not interfere with his son's unsolicited attempt to take the throne, *⁶ (His father had never rebuked him by asking, "Why do you behave as you do?" He was also very handsome and was born next after Absalom.) 1 Kings (NIV)*

Adonijah was an opportunist. He saw an open door and attempted to take the throne. As we will see his attempts were short lived and failed miserably as the true king was appointed shortly thereafter. Adonijah had taken some men previously loyal to the king with him.

Untimely, illegitimate grasping at ruling will always bring division. It is so important for younger leaders not to assume a position that God has not ordained for them. Part of the function of spiritual parents is to help properly align, prepare, equip, and appoint the next generation into their positions of succession.

Opportunistic grasping of leadership mantle will only end in tears and loss!

Thus far, two of David's sons had attempted to usurp their father during his reign as king. Previously, Absalom engineered a dangerous take-over bid that almost cost David his throne and his entire kingdom. (See 2 Samuel 15-18). Although God had raised David up as His chosen king, David had fallen in love with Bathsheba and tragically he murdered her husband and in so doing had opened himself up to a judgement from God, in that the sword would not depart from his house. However, God did forgive David and Bathsheba for their sin albeit there were consequences to their actions.

Adonijah on the other hand, recognised that it was time for a change of rulership and although he wrongly interpreted that the throne should be his rather than acceding that the rightful successor be his brother Solomon.

We must understand that when a father/mother cease to make plans for their children (physical or spiritual), there is a gap created into which the enemy desires to raise up a usurper ruler. A throne is not to be grasped since right use of power relates to the transference of leadership and mantle, marked by the granting of grace to reign and rule in a position of influence and authority for God. Apostolic intentionality must be implemented, or dominion will fall into the wrong hands. Fatherhood coupled with God's governmental grace and power will ensure a smooth handover. David was late and transition was bumpy rather than smooth as the Lord had intended.

I have witnessed dangerous delays in various ministry settings where the next generation have been prevented from taking their rightful place in the proper timeline of God. Delay in generational transition has split churches, broken hearts, and destroyed a lifetime of legacy because the older generation of pastors and leaders failed to recognise their time to transfer leadership. They became churlish and difficult; they opposed the young leaders whom they had previously blessed and identified to succeed them and the young leaders in turn became disillusioned and demotivated. I have pastored several churches through this process. It is not pleasant and can easily be avoided when we walk with humility, foresight, and celebration in the process of generational succession.

Prophetic Insight

Nathan the prophet became aware of Adonijah's actions to become a self-proclaimed king of Israel. The apostolic king David had become a sleeping giant and needed the prophetic insight to release the intended spiritual awakening from God's heart.

Zadok the priest had remained faithful to King David and had also not attended Adonijah's self-proclaimed enthronement. God is still looking for a faithful priesthood to minister unto Him.

Rulership Mantle/Mandate/Apostolic Declaration

In response to Adonijah's actions, Nathan met with Bathsheba (Solomon's mother) and offered his counsel on how she might approach the king. It took the wife of the king, and the man and woman of God working together to release the much needed and long overdue royal edict to crown the new king Solomon, son of David. Despite their previous sin of adultery many years before and all that they had subsequently passed through and suffered in times past, God still chose to bless David and Bathsheba. Now at a pivotal time in the nation's history they were now working together for the sake of the next generation.

The declaration of a king about generational succession establishes the kingdom on earth as it is in heaven. *28 Then King David said, "Call in Bathsheba." So she came into the king's presence and stood before him.29 The king then took an oath: "As surely as the LORD lives, who has delivered me out of every trouble, 30 I will surely carry out this very day what I swore to you by the LORD, the God of Israel: Solomon your son shall be king after me, and he will sit on my throne in my place." 1 Kings 1 (NIV)*

Transference to a Spiritual Son Brings Increase

Finally, David was declaring that the baton would be passed to his son. When leaders make way for the next generation there is transference of anointing and recognition of leadership (note that when Elisha received the double portion of his master Elijah's mantle, the company of prophets acknowledged the transference of leadership and anointing).

13 Elisha then picked up Elijah's cloak that had fallen from him and went back and stood on the bank of the Jordan. 14 He took the cloak that had fallen from Elijah and struck the water with it. "Where now is the LORD, the God of Elijah?" he asked. When he struck the water, it divided to the right and to the left, and he crossed over. 15 The company of the prophets from Jericho, who were watching, said, "The spirit of Elijah is resting on Elisha." And they went to meet him and bowed to the ground before him. 2 Kings 2 NIV

What is especially moving is that the Lord God was so gracious to affirm the transference and impartation from Elijah to Elisha in the dividing of the waters of the Jordan. The young leader needed some divine affirmation to back up what he had received by faith. Young leaders are not so different today.

The Anointing to Lead

Nathan and Zadok anoint the young king Solomon. Benaiah truly grasped the importance of generational succession and the increase that comes with it! *36 Benaiah son of Jehoiada answered the king,*

Amen! May the L<small>ORD</small>, the God of my lord the king, so declare it. ³⁷ As the L<small>ORD</small> was with my lord the king, so may he be with <u>Solomon to make his throne even greater than the throne of my lord King David!</u> 1 Kings 1(NIV)

The successor must take the seat on the royal throne. *Moreover Solomon has taken his seat on the royal throne v46*

David rejoiced in the successful generational transition as He released his son to rule!

⁴⁷ Also, the royal officials have come to congratulate our lord King David, saying, 'May your God make Solomon's name more famous than yours and his throne greater than yours!' And the king bowed in worship on his bed ⁴⁸ and said, 'Praise be to the L<small>ORD</small>, the God of Israel, who has allowed my eyes to see a successor on my throne today.'

There is a timeline in rulership and succession that is ordained by God. When we wait too long, we run the risk of the enemy forcing the hand of an inexperienced power stealer grasping the reins of power. Thrones are not to be grasped. Leadership is a privilege granted in grace.

I have seen this principle of delay cause much damage when spiritual parents delay to step down in ministry. It cause much hurt and frustration for the spiritual children who are waiting to step up and lead. The parents are in danger of moving in yesterday's anointing and the church is not able to move into the news things of God.

The Jesus Generational Succession Plan

Jesus was intentional about generational succession and passing the baton of His leadership to His spiritual children. From day one, Jesus had a succession plan. During His entire three years of ministry He prepared for legacy management, by raising up and training/mentoring a team who could continue the work once He had finished His kingdom assignment, *4 I have glorified thee on the earth: I have finished the work which thou gavest me to do. 5 And now, O Father, glorify thou me with thine own self with the glory which I had with thee before the world was. John 17*

Jesus gave His disciples authority and power to conduct the task before them, to be His witnesses in all the earth. *8 But ye shall receive power, after that the Holy Ghost is come upon you: and ye shall be witnesses unto me both in Jerusalem, and in all Judaea, and in Samaria, and unto the uttermost part of the earth. Acts 1*

His disciples were faithful to the Great Commission that had been entrusted to them to make disciples of all nations (Matthew 28:18-20). It remains our calling and global mission to ensure that the succession plan of Jesus Christ in the Great Commission mandate does not fail in our generation.

CHAPTER 6 - INVESTED

¹⁵For though ye have ten thousand instructors in Christ, yet have ye not many fathers: for in Christ Jesus I have begotten you through the gospel.
1 Corinthians 4

Over the past twenty five years in ministry I have learned a lot about investing in people, albeit I realise that the more I learn, the more I need to learn. One topic that translates into all cultures is that of spiritual parenting, and raising up sons and daughters as the next generation in the faith. Apostle Paul saw it as an apostolic imperative, as we can see by his remarks to the church in Corinth above. With the social media available to us today it is possible for us to mentor multitudes through teaching and lifestyle modelling, however the level of investment we make in spiritual sons and daughters is far weightier and greater in terms of time and input.

Spiritual parenting can be the most blessed of relationships and yet it can also be something that causes deep pain. I have ministered to many fathers/mothers in nations, who have been wounded by spiritual children. I have also ministered to children who have been wounded by their spiritual parents. I have the privilege of having four biological children and many spiritual sons and daughters. Most of them bring me immense joy, but like any parent and child relationship there are valleys and mountain tops. I am also blessed to have spiritual parents in my life with whom I enjoy close and loving relationships.

There are five types of people thus far that I have identified we can potentially invest in as leaders, and these include:

Time Waster

Time wasters are those who want illicit attention. They are the types who come and say, "Pastor my husband/wife doesn't understand me ..." Commit these ones quickly to the Lord and move on. Be especially careful with those who demand your time without others around. Be sure to maintain your boundaries.

Time wasters tend to be either needy or greedy. They are often lonely and have been isolated from any proper fellowship or relational accountability for a long time. They are usually wounded and may also have spiritual issues that need to be dealt with. They may be using their "condition" as a crutch and will often refuse any kind of healing. They are those that usually do not want to be healed. They use the language of "teach me" but in the end remain as unteachable. They say they want to be accountable to you, but by that what they mean is they want to make their own decisions then when things go wrong, they want to have the ability to come back and ask you to fix and/or bless their mess! That is not true Kingdom relational accountability.

I remember once investing quite a bit of time and healing prayer in a young man, but although he got a measure of deliverance each time I ministered to him, the same problem kept resurfacing repeatedly. In the end the Holy Spirit instructed me to walk away because the young man was not interested in getting healed. He preferred the attention he got from saying he wanted to be healed, than walking the courageous path of getting healed. He preferred the comfort zone of his pain than to face the challenges and changes that healing would bring. He was feigning deliverance every time we prayed. I was disappointed to have to let him go but I realised I was wasting both my own time and his. Nothing would change unless he was ready to stop wasting time.

Troublemaker

These types of individuals cause problems wherever they go because they rarely, if ever, deal with their issues so they move from place to place causing difficulty everywhere.

There are profound lessons to be learned when dealing with those we deem as "troublemakers." Some troublemakers are sent by God to hone and shape our characters, whilst others are envoys from the kingdom of darkness with agendas of destruction. I have a dear friend, a Bishop in Zambia who experienced a murderous and serious assault from such a type of troublemaker. The incident involved a woman was a practising Satanist and she and her fellow cohorts were targeting the bishop, his wife, their physical children, and their church. She infiltrated the church by saying she needed help and wanted to be saved but one day she tried to attack him with a knife in church and was intent on killing him but was stopped by the mercy of God and the power of the Holy Spirit. She "repented" and having seemed genuinely penitent the bishop and his wife kindly took the woman into their own family home where they had a young baby. They did not know that she had not truly repented, and the woman tried to kill the child. It is a long and complicated story, but we give God glory for the child's life was remarkably preserved in resurrection in power.

There are other types of troublemakers. These people are adept at stirring things up in churches and operate behind your back saying one thing to your face and another to other people. They murmur, gossip, and complain. Moses had to deal with numerous such types on the journey of exodus to the Promised Land. Every leader knows the type of person I am referring to. We meet them on every journey of faith!

Troublemakers are rebellious. They might exhibit characteristics of manipulation and coercion, as we see in the life of Queen Jezebel, and will wittingly or otherwise bring confusion, corruption of the anointing, sexual problems, witchcraft, and intimidation into church and ministry settings.

A person with a religious mindset will interfere at any given opportunity in ministry to stem the flow of the Holy Spirit, with pseudo religious responses and tactics to power down the church.

A person with character traits of an Absalom-type will kiss you on the cheek, but will eventually usurp your authority and potentially take half your church with them in a church split! Now ALL these things can be changed IF the person is truly desirous of change and humbles themselves, repents and remains accountable. Otherwise my beloved leader, you are wasting your time and they will cause much trouble!

As you can imagine, we do not want to invest undue time in either timewasters or troublemakers, but the reality is you will not know you have a timewaster till they have wasted some of your time or a troublemaker till they have caused some trouble. Discern them quickly, discern the mind of God, plan, and act decisively, swiftly and with mercy. Maintain your boundaries and know that in all God is always desirous to bring forth something of His character in us regardless of circumstances.

Traveller or "Passer-by"

These are the types of ministerial acquaintances we make in a casual and/or occasional or one-off setting. These are people we meet on the way, at meetings, conferences, seminars, and those we encounter as we travel, in passing through places and in life in general. These ones you may only see once or at most a few times in your life. They are migratory. With these people we share some insights concerning the works of our hands in ministry. It may just be a one-off sharing. As a result they may benefit a little from our knowledge, wisdom, and experience but we do not commit much time to such as these because of the nature of our interaction being transitory and temporary. We bless them in some spiritual capacity and then we move on.

Student

Students are those whom we instruct and mentor and disciple to some greater degree than passers-by we meet in life and ministry. We will teach much more to our students. With students we may have them for a particular assignment, or a season of time. We may create teams with students and do Kingdom missions with them. With students we share deeper insights and some more insights and depths concerning our experiences in life and ministry. They have a greater level of access that those we might describe as "travellers" above. We disciple our students.

Students will come and go. Some may go on to become spiritual sons and daughters. Others will be with you only for a season or an assignment. Students may benefit from your mind, knowledge etc. but they are not as close to you as sons and daughters.

Sons and Daughters

Now we turn to the category of those we must seek to identify and invest the maximum time and effort in, to and with because it is our spiritual sons and daughters with whom we will create Kingdom legacy.

It is with our children we will have influence for the glory of God. It is through our spiritual children we will have the most insight, oversight, and partnership. It is with our sons and daughters that we will partner together in the Kingdom to bring transformation in every sphere we are graced to serve Christ together.

[19]*My dear children for whom I am again in the pains of childbirth till Christ be formed in you. Galatians 4 NIV*

Apostle Paul knew what it was to be in pain for his spiritual children and the choice of his words reveal that this was not a one-off process. He was committed to his children. I always smile when I consider how Apostle Paul was a single man who never married and had no experience in giving birth, yet he used this birthing analogy as a powerful symbol for his intercession and fatherhood he invested again and again in the lives of his spiritual children. I have given birth to four physical children and have also known the type of prayer Paul refers to for both physical and spiritual children! Fathering is an aspect of apostolic grace and within apostleship embraces both men and women, albeit we acknowledge and honour the unique place of men as fathers.

We will disciple our sons and daughters, share our heart, mind and ministry and life experiences. We will invest in them in every way, pray for them, model lifestyle to them, provide for them, nurture them, discipline them, direct them, create platforms and experiences for them and raise them up to be all they can be. We will trust them and share almost every part of our life with them. They will enjoy a level of access to us that others do not have. We build and advance God's Kingdom with sons and daughters. With sons and daughters we work towards a legacy, our relationships and real and legitimate and we encourage them to "imitate me" which flows from the trust that comes from deep and genuine relationship.

Spiritual parents must invest in their spiritual children. There is an enormous difference between being a teacher and a father. A teacher will train you for success, whilst a father will teach you and will train you how to be a successor. Investment with the most fruit produced is when it flows from true relationship. It is not "give and give," or "take and take;" it is "give and take" both ways.

- Investing in time wasters, troublemakers and travellers will burn you out.
- Investing in students will bless you and them.
- Investing in sons and daughters will bless them and you and bring multiplication of your spiritual DNA, values, and character, and will birth a Kingdom legacy emerging the next generation to serve God.

As a leader we must have secure foundations and pure motivation. If these foundations are not right, you will end up messing up both as a leader and as a spiritual parent. If there is insecurity in your life you will breed insecurity in your sons and daughters.

Wittingly or otherwise, you will never allow them to attain their full potential because you will be too insecure about whether they will outshine you.

Furthermore, if you have dubious motivation then you will have questionable outcomes. Your motivation will determine your destination. A pure heart will produce righteous fruit, but impure motivation unfettered will cause chaos and pain to you and those around you.

The identity of a son establishes the quality of his fatherhood. The foundation of fatherhood establishes the identity of the son. Sonship and identity in God are the building blocks for spiritual maturation. Apostolic houses build with the mind set of sonship. The government is always on the shoulders of sons/daughters, passed on from their spiritual fathers/mothers.

It is important to understand that there is more than one type of spiritual son or daughter. From my experience I have found they fall loosely into five categories:

Orphan Son

An orphan son or daughter is like a street child. He or she does not know how to receive your love and authority as they are self-parenting and find it difficult to be under authority and are often rebellious. They are insecure and over-sensitive, narcissist and self-ruling. They find it almost impossible to relate to God as Father until they are healed. As a result of not being fathered, they are not able to raise others up to be sons unless they are healed.

Jesus foreknew that the orphan spirit can take hold of any person and He has made provision for healing of "orphan" sons and daughters by way of the Cross. Before His death, resurrection, and ascension the Lord shared a significant moment with His closest disciples, talking about this very topic. *15 "If you love me, keep my commands. 16 And I will ask the Father, and he will give you another advocate to help you and be with you forever—17 the Spirit of truth. The world cannot accept him, because it neither sees him nor knows him. But you know him, for he lives with you and will be in you. 18 I will not leave you as orphans; I will come to you. John 14 (NIV)*

Rebellious Son

These are spiritual children who see your authority and want to usurp your authority e.g. those like Absalom was to King David his father. A son like Absalom is almost impossible to raise up. They will betray you, split your church, try to destroy your ministry and reputation, and attempt to steal your inheritance. I have walked with at least one Absalom type of spiritual son, and I know the damage that can be inflicted on a person and their ministry through this. Nonetheless, I thank God that we learn aspects of love in betrayal that we cannot learn in any other scenario. You will find my teaching in the chapter Beyond Betrayal in my book, *"The Imperfect Leader"* helpful for this topic.

There can be another category of rebellious son who is less like an Absalom and may be compared more being like a rebellious teenager. It is possible to work with these types of children. They simply need love, patience, good boundaries and to learn to submit to a father's authority.

Prodigal Son

11 And he said, A certain man had two sons:12 And the younger of them said to his father, Father, give me the portion of goods that falleth to me. And he divided unto them his living. 13 And not many days after the younger son gathered all together, and took his journey into a far country, and there wasted his substance with riotous living.14 And when he had spent all, there arose a mighty famine in that land; and he began to be in want.15 And he went and joined himself to a citizen of that country; and he sent him into his fields to feed swine.16 And he would fain have filled his belly with the husks that the swine did eat: and no man gave unto him.17 And when he came to himself, he said, How many hired servants of my father's have bread enough and to spare, and I perish with hunger!18 I will arise and go to my father, and will say unto him, Father, I have sinned against heaven, and before thee, 19 And am no more worthy to be called thy son: make me as one of thy hired servants.20 And he arose, and came to his father. But when he was yet a great way off, his father saw him, and had compassion, and ran, and fell on his neck, and kissed him.21 And the son said unto him, Father, I have sinned against heaven, and in thy sight, and am no more worthy to be called thy son.²² But the father said to his servants, Bring forth the best robe, and put it on him; and put a ring on his hand, and shoes on his feet:²³ And bring hither the fatted calf, and kill it; and let us eat, and be merry:²⁴ For this my son was dead, and is alive again; he was lost, and is found. And they began to be merry. Luke 15

The prodigal son or daughter sees your authority but completely rejects it in favour of the world where they perceive a total absence of any authority ruling over them. However, the prodigal child is sure to return if they are truly those who have an experience of God's conviction whilst in the "world." What did the father do whilst his son was gone from him? He watched, he waited, he prayed, <u>and yet he still worked</u>. If you have a prodigal child, you must keep "working" in the harvest fields of the Lord. You cannot give up your work or ministry so that they can be rescued. They must pass through the process of the pig sty to return to the father's arms.

It is interesting to note that we never hear about the prodigal mother; this is because the mother would probably have tried to stop the process. It is a natural thing for a mum to want to protect her children. But God permitted the story to have a father's focus and shows us that a father never stops loving, caring, watching, waiting, and praying but that a father has the fortitude and foresight to know that the young prodigal son must through walk the process of restoration. So it is oftentimes with spiritual parenting.

It is useful to also recognise that there is no narrative after the prodigal son returns and the party is over so to speak. This is my experience: prodigals return home grateful but also often extremely broken, wounded, and weary. They need to be not only reconciled to God and to family, but they also must experience deep inner healing and restoration for themselves from their time in the world. This is where the patience and sweet love of a mother comes in, not to the exclusion of the father because a father also loves deeply, but the mother will often be the one who has the most consistent patience and persistence to believe and work through restoration process with their prodigal child/adult over a period of time.

Elder Brother Son

25 Now his elder son was in the field: and as he came and drew nigh to the house, he heard musick and dancing. 26 And he called one of the servants, and asked what these things meant.27 And he said unto him, Thy brother is come; and thy father hath killed the fatted calf, because he hath received him safe and sound.28 And he was angry, and would not go in: therefore came his father out, and intreated him.29 And he answering said to his father, Lo, these many years do I serve thee, neither transgressed I at any time thy commandment: and yet thou never gavest me a kid, that I might make merry with my friends:30 But as soon as this thy son was come, which hath devoured thy living with harlots, thou hast killed for him the fatted calf.31 And he said unto him, Son, thou art ever with me, and all that I have is thine.³² It was meet that we should make merry, and be glad: for this thy brother was dead, and is alive again; and was lost, and is found. Luke 15

The elder brother spiritual child is just like their namesake in the bible. They are bitter when prodigals return, yet they are faithful to work in the harvest fields alongside of you. These dear ones can be kept from bitterness through our example as a father or mother in the Lord.

The frustration of the elder brother can be seen as five-fold:

1. **He felt unappreciated by his father,** despite his loyalty to him and his work ethic for him. The Scriptures do not record any words of affirmation from the father to the elder brother son while they are waiting for the return of the younger brother. This is not to say that he did not appreciate the elder son, but serves as a reminder to us that it is good, helpful, and pleasant when parents take time to affirm their children. God our Heavenly Father did likewise at Jesus' baptism (Matthew 3:17) and at the time of His transfiguration (Matthew 17:5) Some of our kids need to hear our words of affirmation. It is just how they are wired.

2. **He was tired**. All the time his young brother had been gone he had held down responsibilities, doing the work of two, probably been worried and extremely disappointed

himself that his brother had left and squandered everything. The elder brother, perhaps quite rightly, felt that the younger brother was just a time waster and a troublemaker! To be fair he had a point, but the redemptive heart of God had in mind to redeem the time wasted and the trouble caused. Even the young grow weary but with proper parenting they will rise again like eagles.

3. **He might have wanted to sow a few "wild oats" himself** and quench some fleshly desires, but he maintained a steadfast position of self-control and loyalty to his father's house. Self-denial caused him to become churlish, whereas his denial of self will release the inner peace that presently eludes him.

4. **He was feeling jealous and angry that after all his loyalty to his father, his hard work and dedication that he has received (in his eyes) nothing from his father**. So far there had been no special attention given; no special garments provided, or privilege party prepared for this diligent brother. Nonetheless, he misunderstood how much his father loves and appreciates him.

The brothers of Joseph were angry and jealous of him too, but for different reasons than the prodigal brother. They were jealous of the anointing and the call of God on Joseph's life. In a way, the elder brother in the prodigal son narrative almost had the same problem with his younger brother too albeit it was more subtle, and the primary problem concerning jealousy was more to do with not receiving reward from his father than being envious of the younger brother's anointing/calling in God.

5. **He thought the younger brother had robbed him of his inheritance.** Yet the Scriptures clearly states, *31 And he said unto him, Son, thou art ever with me, and all that I have is thine.*

Despite the trauma prodigal process can cause, it is helpful for us to note that crisis can usher us into increase if we have a Godward response. This is one of the fruits we glean from the prodigal son story. Resilience is a necessary virtue for all believers as it creates determination, work ethic and consistency in us beyond passion alone. Our humble and right response to crisis' can bring forth enlargement.

May we always pray to have eyes that see the best in people, a heart that forgives the worst and a mind that forgets the bad so that we never lose faith in God or in those we love and disciple.

True Son/Daughter

2 Unto Timothy, my own son in the faith: Grace, mercy, and peace, from God our Father and Jesus Christ our Lord. 1 Timothy 1

We are made in God's image and the reflection of Christ through our lives is a mirror that replicates the depth of the love of our Heavenly Father. Our primary example of father and son relationship being modelled is between Christ and the Father. Jesus displayed loyalty, sacrifice, and commitment to His Father's will. These are traits we desire to see in ourselves and in both our physical and spiritual offspring. A true spiritual son or daughter acknowledges our authority and respects it. Genuine submission is birthed out of love NOT out of control. We can never truly understand the fullness of commitment until we comprehend covenant relationship.

Biblical examples of fathers and sons include Timothy and Titus with their spiritual father Paul. True sons and daughters are just that – true and loyal and they remain with us. These are the ones with whom we invest maximum time and investment in every capacity, because with them we are Kingdom building and creating Kingdom legacy for the glory of God. We can send our sons and daughters as our representatives and Kingdom ambassadors for Christ even when we ourselves are not able to go.

We need only look to the life of Christ to see the perfect example of a true Son. The Lord was obedient, loving, humble, holy, and righteous. Whilst our true spiritual sons and daughters may not be "perfect" in all, they are loyal, they are loving, and they trust the grace upon our lives to mentor and disciple them to maturity. There is an African proverb that encapsulates this ethos: better to stand by a dry well with a father than to stand by an overflowing well without.

How Should We Invest in our Spiritual Sons and Daughters?

As spiritual parents we seek to be Godly role models to our sons and daughters. We recognise that our competency as servant leaders comes from the Holy Spirit (2 Corinthians 3:1-6) and that we gain experiential wisdom as we journey through life and ministry ourselves also.

Apostle Paul spoke of being gentle like a mother with those they were delighted to share the gospel and their lives with. He also spoke of dealing with his disciples as a father deals with his own children *encouraging, comforting and urging you to live lives worthy of God who calls you into his kingdom and glory." 1 Thessalonians 2:12 NIV*

Being a spiritual parent is not a hierarchical imposition. It begins with invitation and ensues in genuine partnership and inclusion in the Gospel with those the Lord has entrusted to us. *4 In all my prayers for all of you, I always pray with joy 5 because of your partnership in the gospel from the first day until now, Philippians 1 NIV*

As a spiritual parent or a mentor we have both insight and oversight of the lives entrusted to our care. We invest, love, and seek to inspire them making every effort to ensure they come to maturity. Apostle Paul writes, *19 My dear children, for whom I am again in the pains of childbirth until Christ is formed in you, 20 how I wish I could be with you now and change my tone, because I am perplexed about you! Galatians 4 NIV*

We share revelation and knowledge alongside of our wisdom and experience in life and in ministry. We encourage those we train and mentor to imitate us, as Apostle Paul also did, *15 Even if you had ten thousand guardians in Christ, you do not have many fathers, for in Christ Jesus I became your father through the gospel. 16 Therefore I urge you to imitate me. 1 Corinthians 4 NIV*

We lay hands on our children for impartation of spiritual gifts and for mutual encouragement, *11I long to see you so that I may impart to you some spiritual gift to make you strong— 12 that is, that you and I may be mutually encouraged by each other's faith. Romans 1 NIV*

We instruct our children. Instruction is every bit as needful as revelation, but so much of the body of Christ has become obsessed only with revelation, without understanding that a word of instruction can unlock the miraculous in our lives and cause us to become participators in God's outworking of His plans in our families, communities and ministries, *Give the people these instructions, too, so that no one may be open to blame. 1 Timothy 5:7 NIV*

We teach our spiritual children and model Biblical patterns for them to live by employing discipline where necessary in love, *17Join with others in following my example, brothers, and take note of those who live according to the pattern we gave you. Philippians 3 NIV*

13 What you heard from me, keep as the pattern of sound teaching, with faith and love in Christ Jesus. 14 Guard the good deposit that was entrusted to you—guard it with the help of the Holy Spirit who lives in us. 2 Timothy 1 NIV

We are raising our spiritual sons and daughters to influence, to impact and bring transformation to nations and together we are creating a Kingdom legacy to bless generations of every nation!

CHAPTER 7 - SPIRITUAL FATHERING

[19] Then answered Jesus and said unto them, Verily, verily, I say unto you, The Son can do nothing of himself, but what he seeth the Father do: for what things soever he doeth, these also doeth the Son likewise.
John 5

Having understood that there are several types of sons, it is also imperative that we comprehend there are also diverse types of spiritual fathers' and mothers. One of the greatest needs I perceive the world over is that of spiritual fathers, mothers and leaders in general who need to be healed and discipled to become mature and secure themselves.

We have a generation who are calling themselves "fathers" who have never experienced fathering themselves, and therefore, they are struggling to properly fulfil that role. They are insecure and immature. You cannot truly raise a son if you yourself have never been fathered. It is an apostolic imperative in our day to see a restoration and maturation of the role of spiritual fathers and mothers in the church and in the world. God is our perfect role model as a Father.

Strong Personality is Different from Authority

Personality is not the same as authority. Personality is how you act; it is possible to have a forceful personality and not operate in much authority.

Character is different from personality, because character is who you are to the depth of your being. Character is who you are. Your character will determine the longevity of your life, the impact and scope of your ministry and the type and amount of fruit from your ministry both in the present day and in respect to legacy for the future.

True Kingdom authority has responsibility and stewardship as integral parts at its core. Authority without responsibility is dangerous; yet responsibility without authority is frustrating. Authority with accountability through relationship is a Godly pattern of Kingdom government.

To place a person in a position of authority but not give them any responsibility will cause many problems in church governance. Never delegate a position to someone and then rob them of the opportunity to exercise their God-given authority with those assigned roles and agreed responsibilities. It will lead to demotivation, loss of confidence and can cause a complete break-down in relationship. Likewise, never delegate a position of authority to someone and then not give them any responsibility, they will just become lazy and unwise in stewardship of their 'position.'

To move in authority a person must be under Godly authority themselves. Jesus clearly models this principle. In the fifth book of St John the Lord declares, *Verily, verily, I say unto you, The Son can do nothing of himself, but what he seeth the Father do: for what things soever he doeth, these also doeth the Son likewise. Verse 19*

We are first under authority before God; that is our covenant position as legitimate sons/daughters and heirs and the posture from which we move in Godly authority. True Kingdom authority will always be modelled on the relationship between Christ and the Heavenly Father.

We might view authority in this three-fold fashion:

Authority over means we are responsible for the people whom we have authority over and accountable to God for those entrusted to our care e.g. our congregations, our team members, our disciples, our sons, and daughters, those we mentor and any ministries, or churches or businesses we lead and/or oversee.

As Christ loves the church - may we emulate this love to those we oversee. I have a network of churches that I oversee in a relational capacity, and I also have spiritual sons and daughters who look to me for covering in ministry. I am spiritually responsible for these precious ones God has entrusted to my care.

Authority under means we are responsible to the person or people who have authority over our lives, and we are accountable to same. We are first accountable to the Lord and thereafter to our leaders and/or our spiritual fathers and mothers, apostle, bishop, elders, pastor/leader. May we love and submit to those who have authority over our lives as we submit unto Christ in love. I have two spiritual fathers who speak into my life and ministry as well as a spiritual mother.

Authority with means we are responsible with others and accountable with them in a collective way e.g. those in a team are responsible together and have authority with those they make decisions with. For instance I lead and facilitate a network of pastors and leaders in our region. It is a place of plurality and mutual love, honour, and respect. I am the main visionary for the group, but we govern the group collectively and with consensus and whatever decisions we make we are responsible together for their stewardship and outworking in the region.

I also have several other apostles that I relate closely to in covenant relationship who can also speak freely into any situation in my ministry and life and vice versa, and together with those beloved brothers and sisters I share another aspect of walking together in mutual accountability, respect, and love.

True fathers are kings and priests. They love; they discipline; they provide; they train; they protect; they war; they rule. They are present, they oversee, and they are prophets in their homes and ministerial spheres. On the other hand there are certain types of fathers and mothers who are wounded, immature and/or insecure who can become controlling, abusive, and destructive.

Let's consider some types of fathers, trusting that God is healing and restoring spiritual parents around the world so that the church can attain the full measure of the stature of Christ that Apostle Paul speaks of in Ephesians 4. Let me state categorically that NOT everyone is called to be a spiritual father.

Spiritual "fathering" is not necessarily limited to the male gender, albeit we must acknowledge there is a unique aspect to the role of men as fathers. Nonetheless, "fathering" can be regarded as a function of apostolicity and is this regard is not gender based. We do not minister in our offices because of gender; we minister in our offices because of the spiritual grace and authority given to us by and in Christ. We are neither Jew nor Greek, slave nor free, male, or female with regards to ministry function. It is a spiritual gift to lead, not a gender gift.

Immature Fathers/Mothers/Leaders

As I mentioned earlier one problem, which I have observed and sought to find solutions for is that of immaturity in God's leaders.

One dilemma is that people equate anointing to be an indication of maturity. This is simply not true. A powerful anointing is not necessarily an indication of maturity, because it is possible to be powerfully anointed and still be both emotionally immature and insecure. Maturity can relate to physique, to mental aptitude, to emotions and to spirituality. It is possible to be spiritually mature in the things of God such as disciplines of prayer, worship, obedience, knowledge of the word of God, of the Kingdom, of ministry and yet still be emotionally immature. It is also possible to be emotionally and mentally mature and at the same time be spiritually immature!

Immature fathers and mothers are not capable of raising mature sons and daughters; only mature fathers and mothers have the capacity to raise mature sons and daughters.

Absentee Father

King David was absent from his daughter Tamar's life at a time of terrible trauma and distress. When Tamar was raped by her brother Amnon, David stayed away, and the situation festered until her other brother Absalom took matters into his own hands and killed his brother to avenge his sister. Perhaps if David had been present the situation could have been avoided?

Absentee fathers create insecure children who must necessarily resort to parenting themselves (and sometimes their siblings) in the panoply of life. This situation will always have an impact on life and ministry. Let me stress it is wrong to say you are a spiritual parent to someone and then not fulfil that role. If you are given grace to raise spiritual sons and daughters then please, do it by being present for them (not literally twenty four hours of the day, but just by letting them know you are available and willing to stand with them in any situation).

Too many claim to have thousands of spiritual children, but the reality is they barely know their names let alone their gifting and calling, yet they pretend to be their parents in the Lord thinking somehow it will earn them ministry kudos. This must stop. You can mentor multitudes, teaching and training thousands upon thousands, but to truly raise a son or daughter takes time, effort, and investment at every level and the number of sons and daughters you can raise in such a manner cannot be the same as the multitudes you can teach. In this way we recognise that whilst we will mentor those we parent, we will not be a parent to all those we mentor. Jesus Christ had an inner circle and circle of twelve and of course, He also ministered to the multitudes and in this regard, we take our example from Christ.

A child who has had an absentee father will most likely grow up to be one who has the mindset of an orphan and will struggle with issues of abandonment and a profound lack of self-worth. They will lack direction and may be bitter, with unresolved anger issues. They need constant affirmation and may also have an inability to trust authority figures because the one true authority figure they trusted was never there!

Despite these dire consequences endured by fatherless children, the bible declares that we are adopted into the family of God and that through the Holy Spirit we will cry "Abba Father" to the Lord. We are no longer slaves but sons of God and heirs of God through Christ. (Galatians 4:4-7) Through Christ we can receive the fullness of all that has been promised for us in true Fatherhood. Be patient with these children and model true parenthood and they will flourish and grow.

Abusive or Neglectful Father

Laban is an example of an abusive father. He exploited his daughter Leah by giving her away in a cruel wedding night ruse to be the bride of Jacob, instead of honouring her sister Rachel who was supposed to be married to him. Jacob also married Rachel and the two sisters for a time had a tortuous relationship because of the actions of a neglectful father. We can clearly see that by dint of what Laban did to Leah, he also mistreated his daughter Rachel.

Additionally, Laban maltreated his son-in-law Jacob through manipulation of his time and service, although Jacob was a worthy adversary for the slippery Laban. Remarkably and despite everything they suffered, this family learned to love each other and to re-establish proper boundaries and Godly relationships through time.

A child of an abusive father will have had tremendous fear in their lives and will almost 100% suffer from rejection. They often have a fear of authority, no sense of purpose and a deep mistrust of authority figures. They can struggle with sense of purpose.

We recognise that true authority is given to build others up not to knock them down, Apostle Paul wrote to the church in Corinth, *⁸ So even if I boast somewhat freely about the authority the Lord gave us for building you up rather than tearing you down, I will not be ashamed of it. 2 Corinthians 10 NIV*

One of the great graces the apostolic ministry brings to the church is the demonstration and restoration of true Godly authority and fathering. This brings so much healing to those who have experienced abuses of authority either in their families, workplaces, or church-based settings.

I work with many churches and ministries from different denominational streams and cultural backgrounds. In this last year I have come alongside one church that previously suffered abuses of authority under another apostolic ministry leadership. They just recently shared with me that through my walking with them these past twelve months, they have come to love and trust me because they have now experienced true Godly authority in apostolic functionality that builds up but does not tear down people. Glory to God for this powerful restoration testimony!

Insecure/Immature Father

Insecurity often stems from a lack of identity OR confusion over identity. Moses was suffering from an "identity crisis" and grew up as a Hebrew in the Egyptian courts. When God called Moses, he affirmed his identity within the context of his family lineage. God had to heal Moses of insecurity in his identity. God also had to help Moses to be a father. It took his father-in-law Jethro to speak a word to him in season to help him learn that he could not do all the work by himself. Moses learned to be an incredible leader, father, and military leader and he shepherded God's people even though he was never really fathered in a secure environment in his foundational years. But he could only be successful in all that because God healed him in that area.

Some of the hallmarks of an unhealed child of an insecure father can include that they become "man pleasing" rather than God pleasing; they feed the ego of their father/mother because they are desperate for affirmation. They themselves are insecure because all that has been modelled for them is insecurity from their parent. They are stunted in their emotional and spiritual growth because their parent has the same stunted emotional and spiritual growth also.

They are often jealous of their siblings and suffer from "elder brother" syndrome. They are usually prevented from attaining their full potential because of the insecurity of their father. A person with a father or mother who favours one child over another (such as Jacob favoured Joseph over his other sons) will also be deeply insecure and quite probably jealous.

True Father

Just as in Christ we see the character and lifestyle of a true Son, so also in our Heavenly Father we see the perfection of Fatherhood. Regardless of our earthly experience of fathering or lack therefore, we can find true fathering in the Lord. True fathers' model themselves on our Heavenly Father's character.

Fathering is NOT Spelled T-i-t-h-e

Fathering is not first about tithe. You may receive tithe from your spiritual children, but the tithe is not to be used as a weapon on unsuspecting and gullible spiritual sons and daughters who are not yet mature enough to realise that fathering is not to be paid for. Tithing is sacrificial and flows from love. That does not mean money is not to be discussed between fathers/maters/sons and daughter's not at all, I am simply addressing the erroneous practise of "demand" of tithe for a person to be entitled to call a leader "father" or "mother." It is not right, and it is not Godly to demand tithe. Tithe is given in love and the first precedent of giving tithe is an act of worship in giving to God not to a man or woman.

The tithe is given to the spiritual storehouse. How might we consider the storehouse? The storehouse is where we go in times of need. Spiritually, this equates to provision of cover, counsel, prayer, encouragement, and mentoring.

A *believer* receives their spiritual succour from their local congregation, and naturally should tithe to their church. At this point *leaders* must ask themselves who is their spiritual storehouse, meaning who do they turn to and where do they go for provision, protection advice etc.? Many leaders tithe to their own church or ministry yet they do not receive covering or provision from their churches, but from a spiritual father or mother. I am, therefore, of the opinion that those leaders of churches and ministries whose "spiritual storehouse" and source is a father or mother in the faith, then those leaders should tithe to those fathers or mothers who are their storehouse.

I am a tither myself, and I also receive tithe from some of those I oversee. I give regularly; I operate in first fruits principles, in giving alms and in seed offerings and I endeavour to walk with integrity in all my financial affairs. Giving is not a problem for me. I have no problem with the principle of a spiritual son or daughter sowing tithe into the life of a spiritual overseer, my only issue is when abuse happens around it.

The Bible states we are sons of God through faith in Christ Jesus (Galatians 3:26) and as such, legitimate sons have full rights and access to Abba Father. A mature son will inherit his father's estate. A mature spiritual son will inherit every Kingdom blessing and provision in Christ. Tithing will open heaven on our behalf. If you are receiving tithe from a spiritual son or daughter - give them access to your life.

The promises of God are fulfilled through the Seed, meaning, Jesus Christ (see Galatians 3:16). This principle of promises being fulfilled stands true for all generations in Christ. It is also through our "seed" i.e.

our spiritual sons and daughters that the fullness of what God has promised in and through our lives will come to pass.

A spiritual son or daughter is an extension of the Kingdom values and mission of their spiritual parent. Their relational connectedness produces harvest and good fruit. A father is an example of what to say and how to act. The son replicates the work of his father. *The Son can do nothing of Himself* (John 5:19). This is an example of the blessing and power of covenant relationship.

A father sends their son or daughter in love and reveals all that is necessary for them to fulfil their assignments. This type of "sending" causes the greater works of Jesus to be manifest on the earth, *20 For the Father loves the Son and shows him all he does. Yes, and he will show him even greater works than these, so that you will be amazed. John 5*

A spiritual father imparts life to their sons and daughters, *26 For as the Father has life in himself, so he has granted the Son also to have life in himself. John 5*

A spiritual father imputes and imparts authority to their sons and daughters, *27 And he has given him authority to judge because he is the Son of Man.*

The work we do testifies that we have been sent by our spiritual father *36 But I have greater witness than that of John: for the works which the Father hath* *given me to finish, the same works that I do, bear witness of me, that the Father hath sent me.*

We testify for those we send in the name of Jesus Christ as our disciples. The Father Himself testifies that He sent his Son Jesus (v37)

A father sends their son or daughter in their name. They provide direction and they give covering. Jesus said, *"I am come in my Father's name" v43a*

A legitimate and true spiritual father/son/daughter relationship bears the hallmark of being one in Christ. *21 That they all may be one; as thou, Father, art in me, and I in thee, that they also may be one in us: that the world may believe that thou hast sent me. John 17*

A spiritual parent gives perfect gifts. The bible tells us our Heavenly Father gives perfect gifts *17 Every good gift and every perfect gift is from above, and cometh down from the Father of lights, with whom is no variableness, neither shadow of turning. James 1*

A spiritual parent's love is extravagant! The Bible tells us our Father's love is extravagant, *1 See what great love the Father has lavished on us, that we should be called children of God! And that is what we are! The reason the world does not know us is that it did not know him. 1 John 3 NIV*

A true father protects His spiritual children. Jesus prayed to His Father and asked Him to protect His disciples, *[11]And now I am no more in the world, but these are in the world, and I come to thee. "Holy Father, keep through thine own name those whom thou hast given me, that they may be one, as we are. John 17*

Spiritual fathers' discipline those whom they love. God disciplined His own Son Jesus Christ. *[6] because the Lord disciplines the one he loves, and he chastens everyone he accepts as his son. Hebrews 12 NIV*

Spiritual fathers and mothers provide for their children, sacrificially and in love. God gave us all in giving us His one and only Son, *[16]For God so loved the world that he gave his one and only Son, that whoever believes in him shall not perish but have eternal life. John 3 NIV*

We work in partnership with our spiritual children, providing insight and oversight, teaching and modelling responsibility, accountability, and authority. *[4] In all my prayers for all of you, I always pray with joy [5] because of your partnership in the gospel from the first day until now, Philippians 1 NIV*

We share revelation, information, insights, experience, and wisdom with them. We are inclusive and not elitist albeit we are selective

concerning those in whom we make the maximum investment.

²⁶ *So in Christ Jesus you are all children of God through faith, Galatians 3 NIV*

¹³ *And you also were included in Christ when you heard the message of truth, the gospel of your salvation. When you believed, you were marked in him with a seal, the promised Holy Spirit. Ephesians 1 NIV*

As spiritual parents we invest, love, and seek to inspire out spiritual children.

¹⁹*My dear children, for whom I am again in the pains of childbirth until Christ is formed in you, how I wish I could be with you now and change my tone, because I am perplexed about you. Galatians 4 NIV*

We encourage our spiritual children to imitate whatever they see of Christ in us.

¹⁵ *Even if you had ten thousand guardians in Christ, you do not have many fathers, for in Christ Jesus I became your father through the gospel. ¹⁶ Therefore I urge you to imitate me. 1 Corinthians 4 NIV*

We lay hands on our spiritual children and impart spiritual gifts to them.

¹¹ *I long to see you so that I may impart to you some spiritual gift to make you strong— ¹² that is, that you and I may be mutually encouraged by each other's faith. Romans 1 NIV*

As spiritual parents we given instructions to our sons and daughters,

[19] And he saith unto them, Follow me, and I will make you fishers of men. Matthew 4
[16] All scripture is given by inspiration of God, and is profitable for doctrine, for reproof, for correction, for instruction in righteousness: 2 Timothy 3

We teach them to build according to the heavenly pattern, *[7] Join together in following my example, brothers and sisters, and just as you have us as a model, keep your eyes on those who live as we do. Philippians 3 NIV*

[13] What you heard from me, keep as the pattern of sound teaching, with faith and love in Christ Jesus. [14] Guard the good deposit that was entrusted to you—guard it with the help of the Holy Spirit who lives in us. 2 Timothy 1 NIV

We identify, appoint, anoint, authorise, supervise, delegate, manage, and release our sons and daughter to be men and women of Kingdom influence and impact. To bear fruit for the glory of God, to multiply and advance the King of God and to create legacy in the name of Jesus the Christ.

CHAPTER 8 - PAUL AND BARNABAS

²As they ministered to the Lord, and fasted, the Holy Ghost said, Separate me Barnabas and Saul for the work whereunto I have called them.
Acts 13

Two Different Types of Apostolic Fathers

During a recent conversation with a fellow apostolic leader, we were chatting about several types of fathers, and he briefly mentioned Apostle Barnabas and Apostle Paul. Albeit our conversation was not lengthy, nonetheless it peaked my interest, and I began to reflect on some of the commonalities and the differences between these two great men of God. It is helpful to look at their lives and gain additional perspective on fathering. Thank you, Dr John McElroy for your insight.

Barnabas at Jerusalem (Acts 9)

We first meet Barnabas (whose name means "Son of Encouragement and embraces the notion of calling people together and bringing comfort and conciliation) at the emergence of Saul from Damascus into Jerusalem. Saul attempts to join the disciples, but they are afraid of him and do not believe that he has been truly converted. Barnabas then took Saul and brought him to the apostles, declaring to them how Saul had preached boldly in Damascus in the name of Jesus and how it had been necessary for him to escape in the night let down by a basket in the wall by his disciples, because of the death threats against his life for preaching Christ.

- Barnabas was clearly established in his ministry as an apostle and is a part of the apostolic network in Jerusalem at that time.
- He had favour with the apostles otherwise they would not have listened to his request on behalf of Saul.
- Barnabas was a man of influence, because not only did the other apostles listen to Barnabas on behalf of Saul, but they also accepted Saul into their ministry circle because of Barnabas' advocacy on his behalf.
- Barnabas was clearly a man who was respected by his fellow apostles and a functioning and fruitful member of the born-again community of believers.
- Barnabas was relational in all that he did.
- Barnabas was a networker; he was well informed concerning Saul's brief ministry to date when he presented him to the apostles. He was aware of the fruit in Saul's ministry.
- Barnabas was also a man of faith and saw tremendous potential in Saul. He did not receive a prophetic vision, unlike Ananias, whom the Lord clearly spoke to concerning the destiny of Saul. Barnabas acted only on the fruit he saw and on the faith he had for Saul's ministry.

Barnabas and Saul at Antioch (Acts 11)

As we meet these two apostles in Scripture, the initial order of them being received and sent is that Barnabas is the one who is at the forefront in the beginning of their ministry and missional journeys.

Jumping into Acts 11 we join Barnabas at Antioch. Stephen has been martyred and the church scattered, and the Gospel was being preached by some men from Cyprus and Cyrene who had gone to Antioch to preach to the Grecians concerning Christ. A vast number believed and when this news reached the Council at Jerusalem, they sent Barnabas to Antioch. Barnabas is acknowledged as a good man, full of the Holy Spirit and full of faith (verse 24). The church continued to grow in numbers and in the knowledge of God.

Barnabas then departed and went to Tarsus to seek Saul. Barnabas was a team player, a man of integrity and wise enough to realise that it needed more than one apostle to establish and raise the new believers and the church to maturity.

Finding Saul, he returned to Antioch with him, and the two apostles taught and discipled the assembly for an entire year. They received prophets from Jerusalem, and they also encouraged the disciples in giving and Barnabas and Saul delivered the financial collections for the support of the poor to the elders in Jerusalem. These men were trustworthy both with God's people and in integrity in administration of finances.

At Antioch we observe that the two apostles of God were laying foundations; establishing the church and maturing the disciples. We note that Barnabas is a secure apostle, with no hang ups concerning acknowledging and partnering with the spiritual gifts inherent in Saul. Barnabas exhibited great wisdom and tremendous humility at Antioch. These two fathers made a great and diverse apostolic team.

Barnabas and Saul Sent Off (Acts 13)

After Barnabas and Saul had spent more than a year establishing the new believers at the church in Antioch, there came a moment in God's sovereign timing when the Holy Spirit made an instruction to the prophets and teachers at the church in Antioch, *2As they ministered to the Lord, and fasted, the Holy Ghost said, Separate me Barnabas and Saul for the work whereunto I have called them. Acts 13*

The two apostles then departed from Seleucia, Antioch's seaport taking with them John Mark. They preached at Salamis in the synagogues to the Jews, and then they moved onto Paphos where they were met by a sorcerer known as Elymas. They also encountered Sergius Paulus, an influential deputy in the country who desired to know the word of God. Elymas withstood the ministry of the apostles, endeavouring to turn the deputy away from the faith. Saul, filled with the Holy Spirit pronounced an edict upon the sorcerer, who was temporarily blinded. The result of this power encounter in the marketplace was that the deputy Sergius believed in the Lord and was astonished by the power and doctrine of the apostles.

In verse thirteen we read that the apostles left Paphos going to Perga then Antioch, during which time John Mark departed and left them for Jerusalem. This departure by John Mark would later become such a point of contention between these two great men of God that they parted company for a time because of it. Meantime, they continued their missional journey preaching and teaching.

In Iconium and then onto Lystra, the two men continue to preach. At Lystra a crippled man was healed when Paul perceived the impotent man had faith to be healed and consequently, he called him to his feet. The people were ecstatic and wanted to treat them like gods, naming Barnabas, Jupiter, and Paul, Mercurius, because he was the chief speaker. The apostles rent their clothes and cried out that the people must not worship them but only the One true God who made heaven and earth. It is here in Lystra that we see Paul emerging at the forefront of the apostolic team.

Despite the miracle healing, some Jews from Antioch and Iconium came and spoke against the apostles, and the people turned on them stoning Paul who was left for dead. But he rose courageously the next day and departed with Barnabas to Derbe, preaching and then returning to Lystra, Iconium and Antioch. They encouraged the believers everywhere they went and ordained elders in every churched, committing them into service with prayers and fasting (Acts 14:23).

The Jerusalem Council (Acts 15)

The two apostles were together in a fierce doctrinal debate concerning the issue of circumcision of new Gentile believers with those men from Judea who were preaching a distorted message. They subsequently went up to Jerusalem to the other apostles and elders at the Council there. They were received warmly and shared all that God had done with them as well as the issue that the sect of the Pharisees had raised concerning the need for Gentiles to be circumcised.

The apostles and elders considered this matter, reaching the conclusion that grace was sufficient for salvation and that the Gentiles did not require to be circumcised. They reached a conclusion with Apostle James giving the final decision on behalf of the Council that letters would be written to this effect and that they would be distributed to the whole church by chosen men from their own company including Paul, Barnabas, Judas, and Silas. The bible records they were *"with one accord"* on sending *"beloved Barnabas and Paul." V26*

We note here that Barnabas holds such a special place of honour in the heart of the Jerusalem Council, elders, and other apostles that he is referred to as "Beloved," Wow! Paul was loved, but he was not referred to as beloved here. The Ephesian elders wept when Paul left them on his way to Rome. (Acts 20:37)

The Separation (Acts 15:36-41)

After delivering the letter to the church in Antioch, Paul and Barnabas continued in teaching and preaching the word of God, along with many others including the prophets Silas and Judas who greatly encouraged the people.

At some point Paul suggested to Barnabas they should return to visit the churches in every city where they had preached and see how the people were doing. Barnabas wanted to take John Mark with them, but on this point the apostles fiercely disagreed. Paul did not think it was good to take him with them, because he had departed from them in Pamphylia. *39 And the contention was so sharp between them, that they departed asunder one from the other: and so Barnabas took Mark, and sailed unto Cyprus; 40 And Paul chose Silas, and departed, being recommended by the brethren unto the grace of God.41 And he went through Syria and Cilicia, confirming the churches. Acts 15*

We do not know the reason John Mark left them previously. We only know that he left just after the incident with the sorcerer Elymas. Perhaps it was too much for the young disciple? Or he had other matters more pressing to deal with? Acts 13:13 gives us no indication that it was a departure of animosity. It only affirms that they parted company. Yet in Acts 15 Paul is adamant that John Mark should not come with them in the next phase of the missionary journey. At the same time Barnabas is equally determined that John Mark should accompany them.

Commonalities

Up until now we have seen many commonalities in the two apostles, including, but not limited to:

- They are both apostles.
- Therefore, by dint of their apostleship, they are both fathers in the faith, but they are not the same type of fathers and have distinctive qualities in how they relate to others.
- They are both teachers and preachers of the word of God.
- They are both staunch defenders of doctrine.
- They each have significant spheres of ministry.
- They both report to and work with the Council at Jerusalem.
- They are entrusted with the wealth distribution to the poor from Antioch and beyond.
- Both men are pioneer missionaries.
- They are graced as foundation layers and builders.
- They are both involved in church governance in the appointing of elders in churches.
- God wrought miracles, signs, and wonders through their ministry amongst the Gentiles.

Contrasts and Different Emphasis

With the situation concerning John Mark we begin to identify areas of emphasis that are diverse between these two apostolic fathers. They share many commonalities as listed above, yet there are also different emphases and contrasts in their ministries, which means how they father their spiritual sons and daughters will also look different in some regards. This is a key point for us to understand the Barnabas and the Paul models of spiritual fathering in churches and ministry or business settings today.

Barnabas - An Advocating Father

Barnabas had always been represented as a man capable of seeing potential in others even when everyone else failed to. He was a man of faith. Importantly, without the intervention of Apostle Barnabas when Saul was emerging as an apostle arriving in Jerusalem, Saul could have remained rejected by both the disciples (for fear and unbelief) and by the apostles in Jerusalem because he had no established ministry credibility with which they could assess him. Despite all this Barnabas had the grace, the faith, and the influence to transform the situation for Saul.

Barnabas was clearly an advocate for Saul and without his advocacy I seriously wonder how Saul would have survived those early years of ministry! A Barnabas type of father has faith, powers of advocacy and is a tremendous encourager to their spiritual sons and daughters. They will always see potential in them even when other leaders and apostolic figures cannot.

The apostles disagreed concerning whether John Mark should have joined them on their team. We do not know who suggested John Mark should become part of their first team when they left Antioch, but the two apostles obviously agreed to his being there or he would not have been on the team in the first place. Thereafter the suggestion came from Barnabas to have him join them again, but Paul was opposed. The contention that flared up between them is testament of the passion they both had for the Kingdom and the importance they placed on team ministry. Paul may have been concerned about John Mark's perceived lack of commitment and he was not willing to offer him a second chance. Barnabas on the other hand was willing to put past circumstances behind him and take him on board and give him a second chance.

It is important that we note that there was reconciliation at a future date, and we do not attempt to set a precedent for apostles being in contention! In fact, these two fathers model the principle of reconciliation because later to the church in Corinth Paul writes,[6] *Or is it only I and Barnabas who lack the right to not work for a living? 1 Corinthians 9 NIV*

And in his letter to his son Timothy, Paul writes, [11] *Only Luke is with me. Get Mark*and bring him with you, because he is helpful to me in my ministry. 2 Timothy 4 NIV* [*John Mark]

What glorious testimonies Paul speaks of his fellow apostle Barnabas in team context again and that he also saw value in John Mark as being a potential team member in his letter to Timothy.

Paul – A Governmental Father

Both Barnabas and Paul were types of apostolic father who instructed, taught, defended God's people and doctrine, preaching, and teaching with great power and authority. However, there was a distinct (though not exclusive) emphasis on governmental grace and methodology that we find upon Apostle Paul's ministry that had more emphasis than in the ministry of Barnabas.

Paul's first missionary journey with Barnabas led them to a marketplace encounter and the defeat of the sorcerer Elymas, along with the establishment of the key governing leader in that location in his faith. Paul's ministry is replete with situations whereby he enters the marketplace there to confront and tear up unrighteous foundations and establish the Kingdom of God in instead. Apostle Paul was a governmental father. A Pauline type of father is a governmental father, much of whose ministry influence will be concerning the marketplace. Of course, Paul spent much time establishing government in the church so we in no way exclude the Pauline influence in the church, which is monumental. Neither should we exclude Barnabas from a role in governmental grace.

In conclusion, these two great apostolic fathers shared so much in common concerning their ministries and mission, methodologies, messages, and doctrinal practices. Nonetheless they are two distinct examples of apostolic fathers in the New Testament and from their lives we gain much wisdom, perspective, encouragement, and example in Kingdom living and spiritual parenting today.

Whatever type of spiritual father or mother you ascribe to be, we are encouraged to be the best we can be in service to Christ through the lives of these great men of faith.

CHAPTER 9 - THE PROTOCOL OF BEING SENT

²¹ Then said Jesus to them again, Peace be unto you:
as my Father hath sent me, even so send I you.
John 20

The dictionary defines *protocol* as: procedure, etiquette, decorum, practise, rules, modus operandi, and code of behaviour. These adjectives and functionalities can become a reference point for our study of spiritual protocols falling into broader based categories of Kingdom governmental procedures and practise, conduct, behaviour, and functionality in every sphere of our walk with Christ, both personally and corporately.

Protocol in ministry is important. I am not talking here about who has the most prominent seating position in church, but I am addressing Kingdom principles and procedures that assist us to move in the overflow of God at local, city, national and global levels.

In life we observe rules, protocols, practises, and procedures everywhere and without too much fuss; yet in the Kingdom of God there can be resistance to the topic of protocol as it pertains to accountability, governance, and procedures. Protocol is an apostolic imperative that needs to be modelled and taught by spiritual fathers and mothers.

Taught and Caught

Protocol is rarely taught in the body of Christ albeit some Godly leaders model it. It is a significant Kingdom topic. For my own part, much of the protocol I have learned has been taught by the Holy Spirit, through experiences and through the word of God. But let me also acknowledge pastors, leaders and my spiritual fathers and mother who have modelled and trained me in this arena. Protocol is about honour, plurality, humility, and love and that ought always to be a two-way thing.

Governance and Government

Protocol can be diverse in its expression amongst the body of Christ but at its foundation it is important we acknowledge that protocol is about governance and governmental order, which provides a Godly foundation which, undergirds our understanding. Governance concerns the supremacy and ascendancy of Christ reflecting His power and authority to rule and reign in our lives as we submit to His lordship. Government is about structure and administration of powers of governance. There must be a wineskin in which God's government is modelled and that is the ecclesia (church), the Body of the Lord Jesus Christ.

Prophet Isaiah writes, [6]For unto us a child is born, unto us a son is given: and the *government shall be upon his shoulder: and his name shall be called Wonderful, Counsellor, The mighty God, The everlasting Father, The Prince of Peace.*[7] *Of the increase of his government and peace there shall be no end, upon the throne of David, and upon his kingdom, to order it, and to establish it with judgment and with justice from henceforth even for ever. The zeal of the LORD of hosts will perform this. Isaiah 9*

The devil is always attempting to bring disorder, lawlessness, and chaos to cause the complete breakdown of government and governance. Anarchy is absolute rebellion. God, on the other hand, has given us the perfect model for government and governance in His Son Jesus Christ and through Christ this protocol is outworked in the church of which He is the head.

Protocol concerns the wisdom of God, the love of God and the methodologies of Kingdom principles we live by. Protocol is evidence of faith. It is a system of spiritual values we implement on earth. It is a manifestation of God's authority in and through His ecclesia.

The Protocol of Giving Gifts

Occasionally protocol can be about the giving of gifts. The Magi came to visit the Lord Jesus Christ at His birth and they came bearing gifts. Some cultures are more focused than others on bringing gifts as part of protocol, and this can be a beautiful thing. For instance in my interactions with the Native American people I have witnessed first-hand the love and honour expressed in the giving of gifts, which is a recognition of the grace and anointing upon a person's life, especially if that person is a leader in another sphere or geographical location.

We can see through the example of the Magi in the New Testament that there is an established principle of bringing gifts in the arena of protocol. Now whilst it is important to receive a gift that is well intentioned and given with pure motivation it is also crucial that we understand that not all those who come bearing gifts have good intentions. Some people can have questionable motivation even when they come bearing gifts in the name of the Lord Jesus Christ whether those gifts are physical, financial assets or whether they are spiritual gifts.

Envoys from Babylon

12 At that time Marduk-Baladan son of Baladan king of Babylon sent Hezekiah letters and a gift, because he had heard of Hezekiah's illness.13 Hezekiah received the envoys and showed them all that was in his storehouses—the silver, the gold, the spices and the fine olive oil—his armory and everything found among his treasures. There was nothing in his palace or in all his kingdom that Hezekiah did not show them.14 Then Isaiah the prophet went to King Hezekiah and asked, "What did those men say, and where did they come from?" "From a distant land," Hezekiah replied. "They came from Babylon." 15 The prophet asked, "What did they see in your palace?" "They saw everything in my palace," Hezekiah said. "There is nothing among my treasures that I did not show them." 16 Then Isaiah said to Hezekiah, "Hear the word of the LORD: ¹⁷ *The time will surely come when everything in your palace, and all that your predecessors have stored up until this day, will be carried off to Babylon. Nothing will be left, says the LORD. 2 Kings 20*

In the Old Testament we see the example of a gift being given with a skewed motivation in the gift that was sent by the king of Babylon to Hezekiah in his kingdom. Hezekiah unwisely showed the envoys EVERYTHING in his house; he gave them access to ALL. There was nothing withheld and in truth he did not even know the reason they had come, or the consequences of allowing such people to enter the inner sanctum of every part of his life, and his treasuries, and his palace, and his kingdom.

The prophet Isaiah came to speak with him and delivered the word of the Lord asking him what had he shown them and why? Isaiah was totally perplexed as to why the king had permitted these men such unfettered access. The gifts they brought had disarmed the king to such an extent that he lost sight of all common sense and spiritual discernment. Hezekiah had to reply he had shown them everything amongst his treasure. Isaiah responded that everything would be conducted into captivity in a time to come in Babylon. There were profound consequences for Hezekiah, and we would do well to learn from his experience.

Who is Being Sent and who is Sending Who?

One of the important principles of protocol is that someone is being sent and they are being sent to a person or group of people - and they are always being sent for a purpose, whether that is for good or for evil. We must be discerning and wise (not suspicious and paranoid), but we do have to clear on who is being sent to us, for what purpose and who is sending them. This is an important part of protocol. It reveals relational connectedness, accountability and Kingdom partnership or lack thereof. This is precisely what the story of Hezekiah and the envoys from Babylon is revealing to us.

<u>Too many people and ministers are sending themselves and they have no one to whom they are truly responsible to or in accountability with.</u> They may have some genuine anointing on their lives and some legitimate ministry experiences, but they are not presently submitted to any church or ministry or apostle, or bishop and they are actually "lone rangers" who may genuinely love God, but do not have proper foundations in their lives or alternatively do not have the capacity to fulfil alone the ministry calling they are trying to pursue.

There can be dire consequences of just accepting random "gift bearers" without questioning their intention or motivation before giving access to all we have been entrusted with. I, myself, have had to pastor other leaders through problems caused by such a lack of protocol in a few of the churches with which I am relationally associated. People have received others into their pulpits without due diligence of finding out whom they are connected to and chaos often ensues and/or disappointments occur. We must ask the question: how many churches today open their pulpits and their ministries to people they don't really know? Such ministers come bearing "gifts," but the fact is protocol has not always been followed.

Alternatively, these "sent" ministers may name accountability relationships but often those are either distant relationships that have no depth or longevity to them or worse still they are simply names on a web site or Facebook page. Beloved leaders, please do not receive just any one and allow them to minister to your flocks without doing some spiritual "due diligence."

In legal terms due diligence means the following: reasonable steps taken by a person to avoid committing a wrongful act or infringement of a right or cause an offence. Alternatively due diligence can mean a comprehensive appraisal of a business undertaken by a prospective buyer, especially to establish its assets and liabilities and evaluate its commercial potential.

It will save you much potential pain and problems in the long run if you will follow this straightforward process of due diligence in ministry before you invite an unknown person in your pulpit or church, not knowing their background, ministry experience or true calling. A person who is properly sent will be able to answer all these questions and if they cannot answer them then their pastor, apostle or spiritual father/mother or the person recommending them to you for ministry will be able to commend them to you and answer any queries you may have.

Sending is a Biblical Kingdom Principle

How do we identify who has been sent to us and for what purpose? Our New Testament plumbline for asking this crucial question is answered in the model we see of Jesus being sent from the Father. Christ clearly stated where He had come from and where He was returning to – His Father. Importantly, there was no doubt as to Jesus' declaration that He had come to reveal the Father's love. His source, His origins and His divine purpose were all defined in His relationship with His Father. This is an important Kingdom principle and too often today we do not see this value outworked in ministry. Whilst we can all generally all say we have been "sent" by our Heavenly Father, the reality is that we are supposed to be part of a Kingdom family and community here on earth. When we are sent out to communities, cities, and nations there ought to be a clear mandate from the sending church or covering apostle/spiritual parent.

We note there is a protocol even in the governmental order within the Godhead as we see Christ being sent from the Father. The Lord Jesus always honours His father; He is compliant and obedient to His Father's will. The Son is sent by the Father and then the Holy Spirit is sent after Christ ascends to the

Father. Thereafter the Holy Spirit sends the church on her global mission to disciple nations. We see absolute and total one-ness, connectivity and mutual honour and respect between and among the three Persons within the God head, and yet we see a greater honour being given unto the Father by the Son. So we can confidently say that Jesus was sent and thus established the protocol of being a Son serving who is sent with a specific mission.

Let me add a brief caveat by stating that just because you have been sent does not necessarily mean that you will always be received well. That means there may have been a break in protocol, or alternatively there is spiritual opposition OR you were not sent at all, and you only thought you were to go!

Let me give you an example from my own ministerial experience where protocol should have been properly observed but it was not. I was in Zambia and my host took me to meet a man he respected greatly. We were on the way to visit the Vice President of Zambia and my host was seeking the blessing of one of his leaders. Sad to say the Pentecostal leader that we went to visit did not behave as a mature man of God. My host was gracious and requested the blessing of the leader. The leader whom we had gone to visit put his head down, said nothing, then quietly stood, shook our hands and we left. We were both quiet and thoughtful.

My host asked me afterwards what had happened. My response was that protocol was not observed because the man of God was jealous. His jealousy at our being given an opportunity to visit the VP overshadowed his heart and caused him to withhold blessing. May insecurity and envy never prevent us from walking in appropriate Kingdom protocol. The man had removed himself from receiving a blessing because of jealously. Had he chosen to bless us he would have shared in the reward of our mission. Of course, we forgave him immediately, but his withholding attitude had left him empty handed and hard hearted on this occasion. Nonetheless it did not detract any blessing or good fruit from our mission, glory to God. We had a powerful and successful meeting with the Vice President later that morning.

Breaking Ungodly Protocols

Sometimes protocols need to be broken because the protocols that have been already established are ungodly protocols; an example in the New Testament would be Apostle Paul when he received the Macedonian call. Apostle Paul went with his team to Philippi in Macedonia. They did not know anybody in the city and so they began to pray. They did not just barge into the city; they laid a prayer foundation. They walked as people of protocol observing the location and the people into which they had been sent, praying for them before they began their mission.

Apostle Paul and his team would be used by God to uproot the unrighteous foundations in the city of Philippi, which prior to their coming were gripped by demonic forces operating in the marketplace. After this the Apostle and his team laid new Godly foundations and established Kingdom protocols (see Acts Chapter 16). Humility and the love of God were key characteristics of their Kingdom protocol.

Protocol Creates Righteous Foundations and Breaks Unrighteous Foundations

Proper protocol will always create right foundations and/or honours those which already exist. Where Godly protocol has not previously existed and it is put in place, the new protocol will create a righteous foundation. Where protocol already is present it is important to know and to follow because the foundation that has been established through it will have underpinning values within it.

If you are not aware of existing protocol, there can be genuine and innocent mistakes made but if you do know the protocol and you ignore or break it then you are in effect attempting to build on a foundation of which you are not even aware of its core values. It is therefore imperative to understand that the presence of protocol in a church or ministry or organisation means a foundation has already been laid and you should observe it with humility and care.

There is a relational foundation that establishes protocol and there is also a governmental foundation that inaugurates protocol. There are usually systems and methodologies that accompany protocol. So where we can, we must observe them. It is one thing to perceive protocol, but it is quite another thing to acknowledge and properly observe it. It takes meekness and wisdom to accept that we do not all do the same things the same way. When you are operating in your appointed sphere, you can set the protocol. When you step into another minister's sphere, it is an act of honour to observe the Godly protocol established there.

As I mentioned previously, Apostle Paul went to Philippi in Macedonia, and he created protocol by establishing a prayer foundation. He then broke unrighteous protocols in the city through his preaching and his actions and through his suffering for the sake of the Gospel. There were unrighteous practises operating in the city relating to the economics of the city which were entirely corrupt and driven by demonic sources. Paul confronted these, broke their spiritual power, and was imprisoned with Silas as a result. Their prayers and midnight praise brought heaven to earth and the place became a Kingdom epicentre as unrighteous foundations were destroyed, and righteous ones established for the advance of the Kingdom of God in that city.

When Jesus was praying for His disciples, He requested that His Father protect the ones who had been sent and given to Him. He said, *18 As thou hast sent me into the world, even so have I also sent them into the world. John 17*
21 Then said Jesus to them again, Peace be unto you: as my Father hath sent me, even so send I you. John 20

Having sent them "twice" we can be in no doubt that as disciples we, too, are sent as Kingdom envoys. As sent ones we have favour, a specific mission, protection, and provision of resource. We can see some interesting comparisons concerning the blessing of being sent in the life of Nehemiah.

Nehemiah Apostolic Reformer

In brief, Nehemiah can be described as an Apostolic Reformer who was raised up by God in his day to rebuild the broken-down wall of Jerusalem and repair the gates, which had been burned by fire. At the time God called him, Nehemiah was cupbearer to the king.

Reformers have the capacity to look beyond devastation and see with eyes of faith to receive blueprints for restoration. Nehemiah was such a man. He laid a prayer foundation, fasting and praying and trusting in the power of covenant God had with his people. Eventually Nehemiah appeared before the king and made his request known. There are several principles concerning being sent that we can glean from these Scriptures.

Nehemiah requested of the king that he be given permission to be sent to Judah to the city of his fathers, for the purpose of rebuilding. He knew who he was being sent to, who was sending him and the reason he was being sent. He knew His God and he knew his assignment. He was God's man, in God's time and he asked for favour, and he received favour and much more besides from the king. When we are sent in God's timeline with observance of appropriate Kingdom protocol when too can expect to walk in favour and abundance of blessing.

The king asked Nehemiah how long he will be gone, and Nehemiah set a timeline. *So it pleased the king to send me; and I set him a time. Nehemiah 2:6b NIV*

Nehemiah had the boldness to request letters from the king to give to the governors of the territory he was about to enter. *⁷ I also said to him, "If it pleases the king, may I have letters to the governors of Trans-Euphrates, so that they will provide me safe-conduct until I arrive in Judah?" NIV*

Nehemiah wisely comprehended that although he was very well known to all in his local area as the cupbearer to the king, there were certain places he would enter on his pioneering building journey where he would not be known at all. At such times, the equity of the king's reputation would precede him and sustain him until he could prove his own integrity. When he encountered rulers who would ask who he was, he was able to present letters of introduction from the king. He would be accepted because of his relationship with the king. His mission would be successful because of this relational foundation and would bear good fruit. Not only would it be successful, but it would also be completed in a supernatural period of fifty-two days from conception to completion of the rebuilding work!

I love this important aspect of being "sent." When I send my sons and daughters and those I mentor on mission into territories where they have never been before, I send them with my recommendation and personal endorsement. They do not have to take time to establish relational foundations, because those foundations are already part of their blessing in and through me.

Next Nehemiah asked for resources. He said, *⁸ And may I have a letter to Asaph, keeper of the royal park, so he will give me timber to make beams for the gates of the citadel by the temple and for the city wall and for the residence I will occupy?" And because the gracious hand of my God was on me, the king granted my requests. NIV*

Nehemiah did not ask for all the materials he would need, but he received seed materials specific to his assignment. The seed for the mission came from the resources of the one who was sending him. The seed assets helped Nehemiah to begin his mission and his faith in God would supply the rest of the materials. Nehemiah asked for the specific materials needed for his mission. There is no point going on a building mission with no tools or materials with which to build, yet so often today ill-equipped ministers who send themselves are doing just that! Enthusiasm and passion are beautiful things, but they are not necessarily proof of competency or fruit of experience in calling. Neither are they sufficient to sustain a

Kingdom front line assignment without proper support and oversight.

Nehemiah recognised that he had favour because the good hand of God was upon him. Despite no record of a request from Nehemiah, the king saw fit to send captains of the army and riders with his servant Nehemiah. This is another crucial aspect of being sent – not only is provision made for the one being sent by the sender, but protection is also afforded by the sender. This speaks of oversight, prayer, encouragement and covering for the one being sent from the sender. When I send out teams and sons and daughters with my blessing, they also have my apostolic authority covering them and shepherding them, fighting for them, and defending them, delivering them, and empowering them!

Nehemiah was successful in his mission, albeit he faced intimidation and oppositions from the likes of Sanballat, Tobiah and Geshem. He endured their ridicule, false accusation, and false prophetic plots to assassinate him, but God was with him in all granting his servant great wisdom, discernment, and boldness. The Lord gave him grace to mobilise others to build with him. In the Kingdom of God you cannot be a lone builder, too often people who send themselves are "lone" rangers. Nehemiah moved with faith and authority to overcome all obstacles that came his way.

It is important to note that if you send yourself instead of being sent out by your church, ministry, apostle, or bishop then you are in danger of being overwhelmed by obstacles and challenges, by spiritual forces, by enemy plans, by sheer exhaustion or disappointments. The spiritual atmosphere in unknown territories is different from the ones in which we are familiar, and it is good and wise to have the blessing of a pastor, or an apostolic father or mother as you go forward.

You are not equipped for what lies ahead in pioneering if you are sending yourself. You may have a good heart, an anointing, and a desire to serve God but if you send yourself without the blessing of being properly sent out you place yourself and those you seek to serve in unnecessary harm and cause problems whether you intend to or not. Heaven's protocol is to be sent with a father or mother's approval. Apostolic fathers and mothers are both those who are "sent" and those who have the capacity to send others.

Nehemiah was able to mobilise many people from all walks of life to be part of the rebuilding work in Jerusalem. It is evidence of the fruit of his being appropriately sent i.e. that in being a man *under* authority; he was able to be a man who operated *in* authority. He had a capacity to envision others and the ability to place them in appropriate roles with associated responsibilities within the implementation of his God-given assignment. This is evidence of protocol flow. Those who are properly positioned know how to position others for maximum fruitfulness and success.

Honour and Protocol

Nehemiah finished the rebuilding work and then went on to become a great ruler and reformer in Jerusalem. His obedience to respect and observe protocol caused great honour and blessing to be poured out on and through his life.

Protocol is not about control or abuse of authority. It is about the right use of authority, and the manifestation of the power and beauty of God's governance outworked in the lives of believers. Kingdom protocol brings freedom and blessing wherever it is modelled and observed especially between spiritual parents and their children or mentors and those whom they mentor.

Jesus said, *26 Whoever serves me must follow me; and where I am, my servant also will be. My Father will honor the one who serves me. John 12 NIV*
We see clearly that the Father is introducing the Son; the Son is honouring the Father and then through the Son people are being introduced to the Father and they experience blessing from the Father because of the introduction to and through the Son and by the Holy Spirit. It is relational!

Because of the relationship between Jesus and His Father, the introduction is so blessed and those being introduced are honoured because of that relationship. Who introduces us in new situations can be effective to our functionality, and our fruit in the harvest fields of the earth.

Apostle Paul's commendation of Titus is a helpful portion of Scripture in this regard also (2 Corinthians 8:16-24). Titus was sent by Paul for the honour of Christ. What a powerful and meaningful statement on the topic of the protocol of being sent.

Paul also said of his spiritual son Timothy, *17For this cause have I sent unto you Timotheus, who is my beloved son, and faithful in the Lord, who shall bring you into remembrance of my ways which be in Christ, as I teach everywhere in every church. 1 Corinthians 4*

Paul was sending his son Timothy on another occasion and was concerned that people might not receive him well and so he spoke as a father in defence of his son prior to him being sent. I love this! Not only is important how we are sent and by whom, but it is also vital that we learn how to receive! *10Now if Timotheus come, see that he may be with you without fear: for he worketh the work of the Lord, as I also do. 11Let no man therefore despise him: but conduct him forth in peace, that he may come unto me: for I look for him with the brethren. 1 Corinthians 16*

The relationship between Jesus and His Father is one of honour. It is beyond a superficial or superfluous connectivity. It is a deep, true, real, and eternal. Such Kingdom relationships will always produce reciprocal honour. Honour is never about one person. Jesus shows us that as He honours the Father, the Father honours Him and within that also the Holy Spirit honours the Father and the Son - and from that culture of honour we see in the Godhead, we seek also to operate in the protocol of honour within the Kingdom of God. Honour produces honour. Dishonour produces dishonour. It is as simple as that.

When some people hear this message, they think I am talking about control. No, not at all. Order is not about control. Yes, there can be abuses and excesses concerning outworking of authority but that does not mean to say that we put the baby out with the bath water. It is time for Godly protocol to be re-established in the body of Christ. Whatever your experience or opinion concerning protocol, above all <u>let true Kingdom protocol be about our right response to obey the Lord's command to love</u>. God loved the world so much that He sent his only begotten Son to save us – sending in the Kingdom ought to always be about God's love!

Apostolic Jurisdiction

As I conclude this chapter on protocol and this book on investing in others, I realise that there is so much more that can and must be taught and shared but for now let me end with a thought on what I term as "apostolic jurisdiction." Some people confuse this phrase with the notion of restrictive, territorial expression and expansion in God's Kingdom. However, this is not at all what the Kingdom is about and neither is it the point I am advocating here.

13 We, however, will not boast beyond proper limits, but will confine our boasting to the sphere of service God himself has assigned to us, a sphere that also includes you. 14 We are not going too far in our boasting, as would be the case if we had not come to you, for we did get as far as you with the gospel of Christ. 15 Neither do we go beyond our limits by boasting of work done by others. Our hope is that, as your faith continues to grow, our sphere of activity among you will greatly expand, 16 so that we can preach the gospel in the regions beyond you. For we do not want to boast about work already done in someone else's territory.17 But, "Let the one who boasts boast in the Lord." 18 For it is not the one who commends himself who is approved, but the one whom the Lord commends. 2 Corinthians 10 NIV

Apostle Paul recognised that service in God had "spheres" or regions. He recognised that God assigns these ministerial "spheres" (verse 13-14). He was also careful to appreciate and honour how God had called and used others in His work and that they, too, had a ministry "sphere" (verse 15). It is helpful to acknowledge that our assigned ministry domain is our greatest area of impact, influence, authority, and fruitfulness.

Whilst recognising all this, Paul also fervently hoped that the Lord would enable him to reach beyond his present ministry scope to preach even in the regions beyond the church in Corinth (v16-17). This was not about a wrongful invasion of territory to take over someone else's work. It was quite the opposite. It recognised another man's field of Kingdom endeavour and honoured it whilst at the same time showing faith for Kingdom expansion to pioneer beyond what he or another had already achieved.

The going beyond could be perceived as a territorial statement because it was about advancing the Kingdom in a geographical location. Paul's statement was undergirded with a mind-set that understood protocol within regions and territories, acknowledging other men and women's ministries and Kingdom efforts. Paul spoke with humility acknowledging that only God can truly commend and approve us for effective and fruitful ministry. Apostolic jurisdiction is not built on the spirit of competitiveness, but in the spirit of humility and love with a genuine desire to see the Kingdom of God expand and bring transformation everywhere.

Just as Paul considered others so ought we to also consider this important protocol principle as we "go" in fulfilment of the Great Commission. It is a principle I have tried to embrace even since the early days in ministry.

I remember many years ago I went into Edinburgh the capital city of Scotland where I live. I sought the leaders and said to them that I had come to seek their blessing before I entered the city for the mission I had planned. One of the pastors present was so moved that he wept, expressing his delight and surprise that someone had shown respect to their "sphere" in ministry. It is important that we honour where other men and women have been planted and where they have laboured for Christ. It will not stop us from fulfilling our assignments indeed, it will give us an opportunity to honour those who have gone before us and made a way for others to follow as we acknowledge and bless the spheres of ministerial and apostolic authority.

Wherever you may be right now and wherever the Lord may send you to from here, it is my prayer beloved leader that you enjoy every moment of the journey with Christ. As He sends you forth, He sends you with anointing, with power, with love and authority as His advocates, His ambassadors, and His children.

Our mission and our message is that of the Kingdom of righteousness, peace, and joy in the Holy Spirit.

We are world changers in the hands of Almighty God.

May our lives produce good and eternal fruit and may those we invest in bring great glory to the Father shining like stars as they deliver the words of life!

We are blessed to be a blessing – we, our children, and our children's children yet to come.

To Christ be all glory forever and ever, amen.

ABOUT THE AUTHOR

Apostle Catherine Brown is the Founder/International Director of New Destiny Global Ministries (formerly Gatekeepers Global Ministries), based in Scotland with a global reach. She is a strategic Kingdom builder who ministers internationally working alongside individuals, churches and marketplace leaders assisting them in discipleship, strategising, training, leadership development and community transformation. She is a prolific author and has so far published sixteen books.

Facebook: ApostleCatherineBrown
Twitter: NewDestinyGM
Web: Newdestinyglobalministries.co.uk; transparentpublishing.co.uk
Email: catherine@newdestinyglobalministries.co.uk

Tel: 0843 289 4707
You tube: Apostle Catherine Brown

OTHER BOOKS BY CATHERINE BROWN
(All available worldwide via Amazon)

THE IMPERFECT LEADER

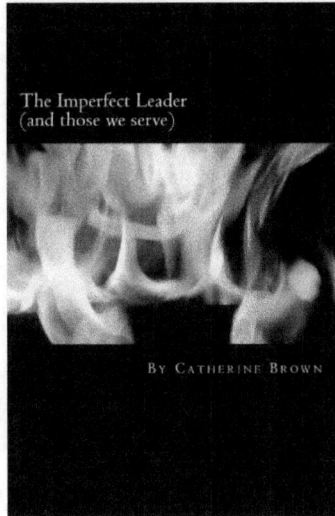

The Imperfect Leader is a must read for every Kingdom leader regardless of their culture, denomination, gender, experience, or lack thereof. Brown skilfully and sensitively unpacks some of the pressing issues that leaders face today, offering invaluable practical wisdom and Biblical spiritual insights as she shares from more than 20 years of ministry experience more than 60 nations.

CHAPTER 1   THE   INCONVENIENCE   OF LEADERSHIP

CHAPTER 2   KNOWING YOU ARE CALLED

CHAPTER 3   PROCESS   LEADS   TO PROMOTION

UNDERSTANDING THE KINGDOM OF GOD

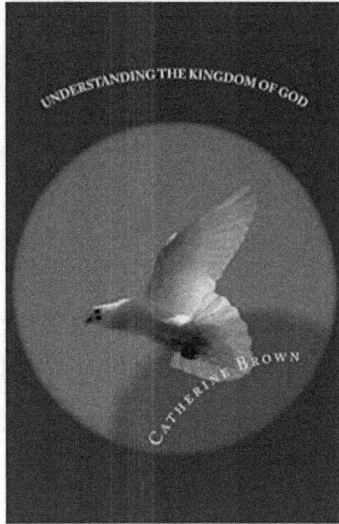

"Understanding the Kingdom of God" is a tremendous Christian discipleship resource for believers and leaders from all walks of life and in every culture. Brown unpacks the message of the Kingdom in a clear and uncomplicated manner, giving Biblical answers to pressing questions: What is the Kingdom? When does it come? How do we enter the Kingdom? What are the signs of the Kingdom? The Kingdom of God is not some high and unattainable philosophical ideal. It is the reality of God in us, God with us, worked out in our daily lives as we walk with and for Him. Whether you are a student or a teacher of God's word, you will not fail to be encouraged, edified, and educated through this Scriptural study. Your life can never remain the same as you seek God's Kingdom!

CONTENTS

SIMPLY APOSTOLIC (VOLUMES 1, 2 AND 3)

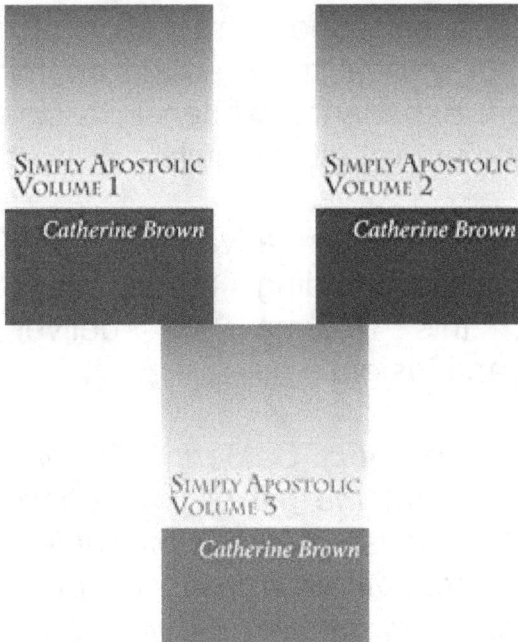

"*Simply Apostolic*" is an eye-opener into the often-controversial world of apostolic ministry. Catherine Brown has written fearlessly and comprehensively on the topic of authentic apostolic ministry, bringing cutting edge insight into the gift and function of apostles and apostolic ministry in the 21st century church.

Respected senior Christian leaders from around the world have endorsed this daring and controversial book. Throughout, it clearly outlines valuable authentic Kingdom principles and practical protocols on apostolic functionality and takes the reader on an amazing behind-the-scenes journey to understand what it means to be a "sent one".

This book is a profound combination of courageous articulation of biblical truth, sound doctrine, wisdom and practical experience written in a clear, concise, practical, and unpretentious style.

For those interested in advancing the Kingdom of God and understanding more about apostolic leadership, this volume will deliver priceless knowledge and insight.

*"In **Simply Apostolic**, Catherine Brown has clearly made the case for the gift of the apostle as one of God's five-fold ministers for His present-day Church. I enjoyed and recommend this book because Brown gives a unique perspective by weaving in allegories and personal stories along with an accurate hermeneutical interpretation and exegesis of the scriptures. Anyone interested in advancing the Kingdom of God and understanding the role of the apostle will gain valuable knowledge and insight.*

*Bible schools and all ministers should consider this book not only as a textbook, but a reference from which to build upon. I encourage and challenge all students of ministry and anyone who plans to be in church leadership to read **Simply Apostolic**."*
Building together with Him and you,
John P. Kelly, Doctor of Ministry
CEO, LEAD (Leadership Education for Advancement and Development)

Convenor, ICAL (International Coalition of Apostolic Leaders)

www.ingramcontent.com/pod-product-compliance
Lightning Source LLC
LaVergne TN
LVHW021507080426
835509LV00018B/2433